Y0-AEW-105

gage
Cornerstones

CANADIAN LANGUAGE ARTS

ST. CECILIA CATHOLIC SCHOOL
355 ANNETTE STREET
TORONTO, ONTARIO M6P 1R3   218

Anthology 3a

gage EDUCATIONAL PUBLISHING COMPANY
A DIVISION OF CANADA PUBLISHING CORPORATION
Vancouver · Calgary · Toronto · London · Halifax

Copyright © 1999 Gage Educational Publishing Company
A Division of Canada Publishing Corporation

All rights reserved. No part of this work covered by the copyrights hereon may be reproduced or used in any form or by any means — graphic, electronic, electrostatic, or mechanical — without the prior written permission of the publisher or, in the case of photocopying or other reprographic copying, a licence from the Canadian Reprography Collective.

Any request for photocopying, recording, taping or information storage and retrieval systems of any part of this book shall be directed in writing to the Canadian Copyright Licensing Agency, 6 Adelaide Street East, Suite 900, Toronto, Ontario M5C 1H6

Researchers: Monika Croydon, Catherine Rondina

Bias Consultant: Margaret Hoogeveen

Cover Illustration: Susan Todd

Acknowledgments

Every reasonable effort has been made to trace ownership of copyrighted material. Information that would enable the publisher to correct any reference or credit in future editions would be appreciated.

We acknowledge the financial support of the Government of Canada through the Book Publishing Industry Development Program for our publishing activities.

7 "At the Top of My Voice" from *At the Top of My Voice and Other Poems* by Felice Holman. © 1970 Felice Holman. Reprinted by permission of Valen & Associates, Inc. / 8 "I Can" by Mari Evans from *Pass It On: African American Poetry for Children* selected by Wade Hudson. Illustration by Floyd Cooper. Text © Mari Evans c/o Scholastic Inc. By arrangement with Just Us Books, Inc. Illustration © 1993 Floyd Cooper. By permission of Scholastic Inc. / 10-19 "I Want a Dog" by Dayal Kaur Khalsa. © 1987 Dayal Kaur Khalsa. Published by Tundra Books. / 24 "My Name" by Nancy Prasad from *The Seasons of Children* by the Canadian Authors Association. © 1979 Nancy Prasad. Printed by permission of the author. / 26-35 "Tiger's New Cowboy Boots" by Irene Morck. Illustrations by Georgia Graham. Text © 1996 Irene Morck. Illustrations © 1996 Georgia Graham. Published by Red Deer College Press. / 38-41 "The Place Where You Belong" from *What Kind of Family Do You Have?* by Gretchen Super. Illustrated by Kees de Kiefte. Text © 1991 Twenty-First Century Books. Illustrations © 1991 Kees de Kiefte. / 44 "If We Didn't Have Birthdays" by Dr. Seuss from *Birthday Rhymes, Special Times* selected by Bobbie S. Goldstein. Published by Doubleday. / 48-53 "A Seed Grows" by Pamela Hickman. Illustrated by Heather Collins. Text © 1997 Pamela Hickman. Illustrations © 1997 Heather Collins. Used by permission of Kids Can Press, Ltd. / 56-57 "Plant Power" from *More Science Surprises from Dr. Zed* by Gordon Penrose. © 1992 Gordon Penrose. By permission of the publisher, Greey de Pencier Books, Inc. /60-67 "Ladybug Garden" by Celia Godkin. © Celia Godkin. Reprinted with permission. Published by Fitzhenry & Whiteside. / 70-73 Excerpts from *Living Things* by Adrienne Mason. © 1997 Adrienne Mason. By permission of Kids Can Press, Ltd. / 76-79 "How Sweet It Is" from *Animal Senses* by Pamela Hickman. Illustrated by Pat Stephens. Text © 1998 Pamela Hickman. Illustrations © 1998 Pat Stephens. By permission of Kids Can Press, Ltd. / 82-84 "Bugs! Bugs!" and "Spaghetti Seeds" from *A Pizza the Size of the Sun* by Jack Prelutsky. © 1994, 1996 by Jack Prelutsky. By permission of Greenwillow Books, a division of William Morrow & Company, Inc. / 87 "Winter Weather Watch" from *Eenie Meenie Manitoba* by Robert Heidbreder. © 1996 Robert Heidbreder. By permission of Kids Can Press, Ltd. / 88-97 "Very Last First Time" by Jan Andrews. Illustrations by Ian Wallace. Text © 1985 Jan Andrews. Illustrations © 1985 Ian Wallace. A Groundwood Book/Douglas & McIntyre. / 100-102 Excerpts from *Who Hides in the Park?* by Warabé Aska. © 1996 Warabé Aska. Published by Tundra Books. / 114-125 "The Fishing Summer" by Teddy Jam. Illustrated by Ange Zhang. Text © 1997 Teddy Jam. Illustrations © 1997 Ange Zhang. A Groundwood Book/Douglas & McIntyre. / 128 "The Circle of Thanks" from *The Circle of Thanks: Native American Poems and Songs of Thanksgiving* told by Joseph Bruchac. © 1996 Joseph Bruchac.

Published by Bridge Water Books. / 131 "Open a Book" from *Pass the Poems Please* by Jane Baskwill. © 1989 Jane Baskwill. Published by Wildthings Press. / 132-135 "Elephant and Hare" from *Crow & Fox* by Jan Thornhill. © 1993. By permission of the publisher, Greey de Pencier Books, Inc. / 138-145 "Kitoto the Mighty" by Tololwa M. Mollel. Illustrated by Kristi Frost. Text © 1998 Tololwa M. Mollel. Illustrations © 1998 Kristi Frost. By permission of Stoddart Publishing Co. Ltd. / 150-157 "Cinderella Penguin" by Janet Perlman. © 1992 Janet Perlman. By permission of Kids Can Press, Ltd.

Photo Credits

22 Tundra Books; 36, 36-37, 105 Calgary Exhibition & Stampede; 56-57 69 Dave Starrett; 70, 72-73, 75 Ray Boudreau; 71 Publiphoto/Eye of Science/Science Photo Library; 98-99 Bryan and Cherry Alexander/First Light; 104 Jean R. Kemp/VALAN PHOTOS; 106 Mike Macri/Masterfile; 107 Norman Piluke/Canada In Stock/Ivy Images; 108 Bob Chambers/Canada In Stock/Ivy Images; 109 Lorraine Pasow/Chisholm Film/Canad In Stock/Ivy Images; 110 Dan Roitner/Canada In Stock/Ivy Images; 111 Roman Jaskolski/VALAN PHOTOS; 148 Richard Woolner/© Tololwa Mollel.

Illustrations

6-7 Philippe Béha; 21, 103, 146 Dayle Dodwell; 22, 23 **right** Dayal Kaur Khalsa/Tundra Books; 23 **left** Georges Seurat; 42-43 Jack McMaster; 46-47 Brian Stewart; 54-55 Margaret Hathaway; 56, 59 Tina Holdcroft; 69 Linda Stephenson; 81, 137 Bill Suddick; 86-87 Joe Weissman; 112-113 Stephen Harris; 127 Jun Park; 128 Murv Jacob; 130-131 Martin Springett; 149 **top left** Paul Morin/Oxford University Press, **bottom left** Barbara Spurll/Stoddart Publishing Company, **right** Kathy Blankley/Lester Publishing, Ltd.; 159 Steve Attoe.

Canadian Cataloguing in Publication Data

Main entry under title:

Gage cornerstones: Canadian language arts. Anthology

Writing team: Christine McClymont, et al.
ISBN 0-7715-1198-1

1. Readers (Elementary).   I. McClymont, Christine.
II. Title: Cornerstones: Canadian language arts.
III. Title: Anthology, 3a

PE1121.G27 1998   428.6   C98-932139-8

ISBN 0-7715-**1198**-1
  4 5 6 BP 03 02 01
Printed and bound in Canada.

Cornerstones Development Team

HERE ARE THE PEOPLE WHO WORKED HARD TO MAKE THIS BOOK EXCITING FOR YOU!

WRITING TEAM

Christine McClymont
Patrick Lashmar
Dennis Strauss
Josephine Lashmar
Patricia FitzGerald-Chesterman
Cam Colville
Robert Cutting
Stephen Hurley
Luigi Iannacci
Oksana Kuryliw
Caroline Lutyk

GAGE EDITORIAL

Joe Banel
Rivka Cranley
Elizabeth Long
Evelyn Maksimovich
Diane Robitaille
Darleen Rotozinski
Jennifer Stokes
Carol Waldock

GAGE PRODUCTION

Anna Kress
Bev Crann

DESIGN, ART DIRECTION & ELECTRONIC ASSEMBLY

Pronk&Associates

ADVISORY TEAM

Connie Fehr Burnaby SD, BC
Elizabeth Sparks Delta SD, BC
John Harrison Burnaby SD, BC
Joan Alexander St. Albert PSSD, AB
Carol Germyn Calgary B of E, AB
Cathy Sitko Edmonton Catholic SD, AB
Laura Haight Saskatoon SD, SK
Linda Nosbush Prince Albert SD, SK
Linda Tysowski Saskatoon PSD, SK
Maureen Rodniski Winnipeg SD, MB
Cathy Saytar Dufferin-Peel CDSB, ON
Jan Adams Thames Valley DSB, ON
Linda Ross Thames Valley DSB, ON
John Cassano York Region DSB, ON
Carollynn Desjardins
　　　Nipissing-Parry Sound CDSB, ON
David Hodgkinson Waterloo Region DSB, ON
Michelle Longlade Halton CDSB, ON
Sharon Morris Toronto CDSB, ON
Heather Sheehan Toronto CDSB, ON
Ruth Scott Brock University, ON
Elizabeth Thorn Nipissing University, ON
Jane Abernethy Chipman & Fredericton SD, NB
Carol Chandler Halifax Regional SB, NS
Martin MacDonald Strait Regional SB, NS
Ray Doiron University of PEI, PE
Robert Dawe Avalon East SD, NF
Margaret Ryall Avalon East SD, NF

Contents

All About Me

At the Top of My Voice

Poem by Felice Holman

When I stamp
The ground thunders,
When I shout
The world rings,
When I sing
The air wonders
How I do such things.

I Can

I can
be anything
I can
do anything
I can
think
anything
big
or tall
OR
high or low
W I D E
or narrow
fast or slow
because I
CAN
and
I
WANT
TO!

Poem by **Mari Evans**

Picture by **Floyd Cooper**

Personal Response

- The poet says, "I can do anything."
  What do you want to do?
  What do you want to be?

- Here are some words about feelings:

  proud   sad   happy   mad   stubborn

  Which of these words show how the poet feels?
  What other words could you use?

- With a partner, read the poem out loud.
  Remember how the poet is feeling.

ALL ABOUT ME

Copy this list onto a piece of paper.
Fill it in with answers that tell "all about me!"

When you've finished, share your list with a classmate. Ask each other questions about your favourite things. Then the whole class can pin their lists to a big display board called "All About Us!"

Name _____

All About Me

My Favourite Books—

My Favourite Foods—

TV Shows I Like—

Sports I Like—

Games I Like To Play—

Clubs I Belong To—

Special Lessons—

Have you ever wanted something you couldn't have? How did you try to get it?

Story and Pictures by
Dayal Kaur Khalsa

I Want a Dog

May wanted a dog more than anything else in the world. She thought about dogs all the time. She talked about dogs; she made drawings of dogs; she read books about dogs. The walls of her room were completely covered with pictures of dogs. But every time she asked her parents if she could have a dog, they said, "No."

It seemed as if everyone else in the world had a dog except May. This made her want one even more.

She wanted a dog to play with and to take to the park. She wanted a dog to take care of— to brush and bathe and feed dog biscuits to. But most of all, she wanted to feel the tug of a dog on a leash.

May told her parents that a dog would be good for the whole family.

A dog could chase away robbers, fetch the evening paper, and bring them their slippers. A dog could even be taught to shake hands.

But no matter what reasons she gave, still they always said, "We're sorry, May, but not now. You can have a dog when you're older." May, though, wanted a dog *right now*.

As she sat in school daydreaming about dogs, May had a great idea. If she could show her parents how much dogs were attracted to *her,* maybe they would get her one.

When she got home that afternoon she ran right to the refrigerator and grabbed a thick slice of salami. She went outside and began strolling slowly down the street. Every dog on the block jumped up as May walked by.

By the time she had gone all the way around the block there was a whole herd of hungry dogs trailing behind her. May was very happy. *Ten* dogs!

"They followed me, Ma," she explained when she got home. "Dogs just seem to want to be with me."

Her mother was not fooled. She told May to use the same technique to lead all the dogs back where they belonged.

May was disappointed but not discouraged. She remembered when she had first tried to roller-skate. She kept falling down, but her father told her, "If at first you don't succeed, try, try, try again."

And that's what she had always done. Now she *could* roller-skate. May decided to try another way to get a dog.

For this one she needed to save up all her allowance. When the day she had been planning finally arrived, she went out and bought everything she needed: a birthday cake, candles, a birthday card, and— a puppy!

When May got home she set everything up on the kitchen table.

"Ma, come quick!" she yelled. Her mother rushed into the kitchen.

"Surprise! Happy Birthday!" May shouted, pointing to a big brown box.

"What can this be?" her mother asked as she pushed the flaps aside.

A little spotted puppy poked his head out and licked her hand. "I bought you a friend," said May.

At first her mother was too surprised to speak. Then she turned to May, patted her on the shoulder, and said, "Nice try, but not now."

She called a taxi so May could take the puppy right back to the pet store.

May kept repeating to herself, "Try, try, try again."

That evening her parents decided it was time to settle the dog question once and for all. They sat down in the living room and explained to May why they didn't want her to have a dog now.

Her mother began.
"Dogs take a lot of care."
"I'll do it," said May.

"They have to be walked every morning and every night," her father said. "In rain and sleet and hail and snow."

"I'll do it," said May.

"Dogs have to be brushed and bathed and taken to the vet for shots," her mother said.

"I'll do it," said May.

"Dogs have to be trained to obey," said her father.

"I'll do it *all*," said May, for every reason they gave for *not* wanting a dog was exactly why she *did* want a dog.

They had a lot of other reasons as well. Nevertheless, May pleaded, "Please, please, please, *please,* can I have a dog anyway?" But still her parents said, "No."

May was furious. She stomped up to her room, and threw her toys all over the place. She kicked her roller skate with all her might. It whipped out the door, raced across the hall to the top of the stairs, plunged over, and bumped all the way to the bottom.

May watched in amazement. The roller skate looked like a little white dog bounding down the stairs.

May had a great idea.

She tied a rope around the roller skate and pulled. The roller skate rolled toward her. She walked across the room with it. The roller skate rolled after her. It was just like walking a dog on a leash.

May went to work. She built a giant training course where she could practise walking her roller skate.

"**W**e're so happy to see you busy doing something other than always trying to get a dog," her parents told her.

When she could walk the roller skate across cracks and around corners without the roller skate tumbling, May felt ready to try it outside.

The roller skate bumped over the sidewalk like a frisky little puppy. When May ran fast and stopped short, the roller skate shot ahead of her, tugging on the leash. It was almost like having a real dog.

But when she took her roller skate to the playground, her friends laughed. They said she looked funny dragging a roller skate around on a rope.

"It's not a rope," she said. "It's a leash. I'm practising for when I get a real dog. And then I'm only going to let people who *really* know how to walk a dog, walk mine."

A fter that, they all wanted to walk her roller skate.

Her roller skate went with her everywhere. But wherever it said **No Dogs Allowed**, she left it outside, tied to a tree.

On the day the new comic books arrived at Sam's Luncheonette, May could hardly wait to get there. She ran to the store, tossed her roller skate's leash around a tree, and rushed in.

While she was busy deciding which comic book to buy, outside on the street a big dog trotted up to the roller skate and began sniffing it all over. He nudged it with his nose.

The leash slipped. He grabbed the roller skate in his huge mouth and ran away with it.

Imagine how May felt when she came out— and the roller skate was gone!

She looked for it all over: in doorways, under cars, behind hedges. She stopped people and asked, "Have you seen a roller skate on a leash?" But no one had.

May felt miserable. It was almost like losing a real dog. She turned toward home, all alone.

Then she remembered those old familiar words: Try, try, try again. So she kept on looking. Even in garbage cans.

She finally found it—scratched and dirty— a block away. She hugged the roller skate tight and carried it home and cleaned it up just like new.

After that, May and her roller skate were never far apart. She even took it trick or treating.

And every day, in rain or sleet or hail or snow, May took her roller skate for a walk.

Her parents were very impressed. "We can see that when you get a real dog, you'll know how to take good care of it," they said.

In a couple of years, May did get a real dog of her own. Meanwhile, though, May, and all her friends, kept on practising.

May tries many
different ways
to get a dog.
Which way do
you like best?

Understanding the Story

Nothing Like a Dog!

- What is the biggest reason why May wants a dog?
- What reasons do May's parents give for saying, "No"?
- May tries three ways to convince her parents to let her have a dog. Make up a title for each of the three ways.
- What surprising things happen after May starts walking her roller skate?
- Do you think the ending of the story is a happy ending? Explain your answer.

**Congratulations!
You've read the
whole story!**

WRITING IN YOUR JOURNAL

In your journal, finish the sentence "I want a..." Now tell a story about the thing you want. Do your parents want you to have this? What will you do to try and get it? Will you have fun trying?

The author of this story also painted the pictures. Some of them have very funny details— like the picture of May daydreaming in class about dogs. Get together with a partner, and make a list of the funny details in these pictures. Share your list with other classmates.

Read this story with your family. Show them your favourite picture.

Read about Dayal Kaur Khalsa on page 22.

Create a Brochure

HOW TO CARE FOR A DOG

Caring for a dog is a great responsibility. Do you help to take care of a dog at home? What do you do to help?

- Write a list of rules for "How to Care for a Dog." Use your own ideas, and ideas from the story.

- Collect some photos of dogs from old magazines. If you can use a camera, take some photos of dogs. Show the dogs doing lots of different things.

- Put your list and photos together to make a brochure.

MEET AUTHOR AND ARTIST

Dayal Kaur Khalsa

. . . .

Profile by Susan Hughes

When she was a girl, Dayal Kaur Khalsa (pronounced like *Dye-yal Kar Kal-sa*) had a dream. She wanted a dog. In fact, she wanted two dogs. She even knew what she would name her dogs: Ginger and Pedro. But try as she might, she couldn't persuade her mother to let her have even one dog.

That's why—years later—Dayal wrote the book *I Want a Dog.* She remembered how much she had wanted a dog. She decided to use her childhood feelings and invent a story. Of course, because she was a writer, Dayal knew she didn't have to write exactly what happened in real life. So she happily let May convince her parents to get her a dog—some day.

Dayal wanted to be a cowboy and an artist when she grew up. She never became a cowboy—but that is why she wrote her book *Cowboy Dreams*. Again, she used her memory of how she felt as a child to come up with a wonderful story. Her book shows things she would have done if she could have been a cowboy.

Dayal was an artist as well as an author. In fact, she illustrated almost all her own books. She would usually begin a story by making a list of all the pictures she wanted to do. Then she would paint the illustrations. Only then would she write the story!

Dayal's illustrations are full of jokes. She used some of the world's famous paintings to help her. For example, the cover of *I Want a Dog* is actually a fun imitation of a painting by a French artist named Seurat. The original painting is called *Sunday Afternoon on the Island of La Grande Jatte*—and it only has two dogs in it. Look at the two paintings side by side and it may make you giggle!

My Name

Poem by Nancy Prasad

Pictures by Scot Ritchie

Lately I have been
Writing my name
Over and over again.

I put it in books
And all over
Empty pieces of paper.
I cover my hands and my desk.

Everything that belongs to me
Or might belong to me
I quickly claim
With my name.

I try all the different
Shapes and forms of letters
To show the power in it, its beauty
I bring out with pencils and ink.

My name! My name!
In time it will tell me
Who I really am.

Personal Response

- How do you feel when you write your name? Where do you write your name?
- What do you think the last three lines of the poem mean?

    "My name! My name!
    In time it will tell me
    Who I really am."

Find Out More About...

Find out more about your name. Use books from the library to find out what your name means. Ask your parents or guardian to tell you how you got your name. Share the story of your name with your classmates.

Make a Signature Board

How many ways can you write your name? Try writing it with crayons, pencils, and markers. Try different colours and shapes of letters. Then choose the way you like best. That's your signature! On a large piece of poster paper, you and all your classmates can sign your names. Add pictures of yourselves.

You and your family could make a signature board at home.

Did you ever wear something new and nobody noticed? That's what happens to Tyler (nicknamed Tiger) in this story.

Tiger's New Cowboy Boots

Story by
Irene Morck

Pictures by
Georgia Graham

Tyler finally had real cowboy boots. Other years on the cattle drive he'd had to wear running shoes. Nobody wore runners on a cattle drive. Nobody but Tyler, the city kid.

"Woo-ee!" said the salesman. "The cowpokes are gonna be jealous of your boots."

Especially Jessica, thought Tyler. None of her cowboy boots ever looked this good.

It was a long bus ride to Uncle Roy's ranch. But Tyler's boots felt as soft as a pony's nose. He drifted asleep with the sweet smell of new leather.

At sunrise, the lady sitting beside him said, "Oh my, what nice cowboy boots."

"I have to help herd cattle to their summer pasture today," said Tyler. He could hardly stop smiling.

The lady took out a thermos of coffee. The bus hit a bump. Oh no!

"My boots!" cried Tyler.

∩ ∩ ∩

"Hi, little Tiger," said the cowhand who picked him up at the bus station. "Good thing you came to help. Only six of us riding on this year's drive."

He never noticed Tyler's new boots. Maybe it was too early in the morning. Or maybe there was too much stuff in the truck.

"Four hundred cows and calves," said the cowhand when they stopped above Misty Valley Ranch. "Sure hope we can make them swim the river."

Tyler nodded. He bent to wipe the dust off his boots. The cowhand still didn't notice.

Everyone was waiting. Jessica, Tyler's cousin, had a horse already saddled for him.

"Let's get these cattle moving," said Uncle Roy. "It's going to be a long hot twenty kilometres to the river."

Cows bellowed to their calves. Calves bawled back. People hollered.

"Hey, Jessica," said Tyler, "did you see my..."

But she was already riding away. "Ee-YAAAW! Ee-YAAAW! Ee-YAAAW!"

The Orphan Calf

At the first steep hill the cattle stopped. They didn't want to climb. The riders and horses had to work hard. The cattle started scrambling up the hill—most of them.

A calf darted from the herd. "Get her, Tiger!" yelled one of the cowhands.

Tyler lunged his horse and turned the calf back.

"Poor little critter," said Jessica. "She doesn't care about staying with the rest of the herd. Her mother died last week."

Some cattle tried veering off the trail to hide from the cowhands or the burning sun. Riders chased them back. The forest was deep. You could get lost in no time. "Ee-YAAAW! Ee-YAAAW! Ee-YAAAW!"

Tyler wiped the sweat from his dusty face. When he looked up, the orphan calf was gone.

Branches brushed against Tyler's head, and whacked him in the face. He felt scared. Finally Tyler found the calf panting under a bush.

"Get up!" he shouted.

The calf didn't move.

"I'm sorry about your mother," said Tyler, "but we've gotta find the trail again."

The animal just stared.

"Everybody's left us!" Tyler yelled.

Angry now, he jumped off his horse to crawl into the bush after her. With all his strength, he shoved the calf through the tangled branches.

He tripped over a branch, cutting a deep jagged scratch across his boot. But there wasn't time to even think about that now.

The cattle drive wore on. The smallest calves shuffled farther and farther behind. Tyler felt dizzy from hunger and heat.

They reached a clearing. At last everyone could rest. The cattle lay down, too tired to moo.

Time for lunch.

Mustard squirted from Tyler's sandwich. He jumped back and stepped in something worse. Yuck!

Would Jessica—or anybody—see these boots before they were completely wrecked?

"Maybe this heat will make the cattle want to swim," said a cowhand.

"It's swim or a mighty long truck ride," said Uncle Roy. The nearest bridge was a hundred kilometres away. Bounced for hours over gravel roads last year, eight calves got sick with shipping fever.

And you could buy a hundred pairs of cowboy boots for what Uncle Roy would have to pay to truck the cattle.

River Crossing

After their rest, the herd moved on again.
About two o'clock they reached a creek. The animals
strode into the cool water. This creek wasn't deep
or wide like the big river—the river that had drowned
a calf one year.

Tyler lifted his feet so the creek water couldn't
splash his boots. Wet leather would dry all stiff
and dull.

"Hey, Tyler. Watch out!" Jessica was shouting.
"Your friend is escaping again."

"Some friend," said Tyler, heading after the
orphan calf. "Call her Trouble."

"There's the river!" said Jessica. "Wow, it's higher
than normal. Must have been raining a lot up in the
mountains."

The river looked real scary. But first they had to
chase all four hundred cattle into the huge holding
corral on the river bank.

When the cows and calves were trapped, ready for the crossing, Uncle Roy barked out orders to get everyone in place.

"Tyler," he said, "you stand with your horse in the water—right beside that panel. Don't let any cattle escape around it."

A cowhand opened the gate for three cows to lead the way. Riders, hollering, chased them toward the water.

The first cow plunged in, surfaced, and started swimming. Everybody whooped and cheered.
The second cow hit the water.

Tyler didn't realize the current was pulling his horse downstream. The third cow noticed a space widening between the panel and Tyler's horse. The cow slipped past and charged up the bank.

Tyler raced after her. In the confusion, the first two cows turned and swam back. They got away, too.

By the time those three cows were rounded up, it was after five o'clock. Tyler couldn't bear to look

at anyone. He'd let them down.

When the crossing started again, he kept his horse tight against the panel.

"No getting by me this time," he muttered to himself.

Suddenly the cattle were swimming! Calves disappeared under the water, then bobbed up, wide-eyed, snorting and struggling. Somehow each one figured out how to swim.

Needing every bit of energy, cows and calves swam silently. On the other bank, the cattle scrambled up, dripping wet, bawling again.

Tyler forced the few remaining calves toward the water. At last they jumped in. All except one. Little Trouble.

Yelling, he crowded his horse against the trembling calf, but she was too scared to jump in.

Tyler leaped off his horse. He sloshed through the water and mud. Before the startled riders could say a thing, he was shoving Trouble down the bank, her tiny hooves skidding every which way.

His muscles ached, but Tyler kept pushing and heaving until that calf tumbled—splash!— into the river.

"Way to go, Tiger!" shouted Uncle Roy.
Jessica grinned.

Tyler vaulted onto his horse to follow Trouble.
Ice-cold water flooded his boots.

He kept his horse swimming right beside the calf,
terrified each time her face disappeared under the
water, thrilled each time it reappeared.

"Ee-YAAAW! Ee-YAAAW! Ee-YAAAW!" he hollered.
"We're almost there!"

Beyond the river, time disappeared in a blur.
Tyler's wet jeans started to dry. The water in his boots
warmed up and felt good sloshing between his toes.

Finally the herd reached their summer meadow.

Tyler collapsed in the grass, almost too tired to speak.

"Wow—check it out," said one of the cowhands. "Tiger's got real cowboy boots."

Tyler looked at his muddy, stained, soggy, cut-up boots. "They're real all right," he said, half-smiling. "Maybe...too real."

Jessica trudged over to Tyler and flopped down beside him.

"Hey, Tiger," she said, "your boots are just like mine."

FOLLOW UP

Would you like to go on a cattle drive like Tyler does? What was the best part of the drive, in your opinion?

Understanding the Story

Call Her Trouble?

- Why is Tyler, the city kid, so excited about his new cowboy boots?

- Do you think his cousin Jessica is a city kid, too? Explain your answer.

- What is Tyler's special job on the cattle drive? What makes it a tough job?

- How does Tyler feel as his boots keep getting muddy and scratched?

- At the end of the story a cowhand says, "Tiger's got real cowboy boots." Is real better than new? Why?

Find Out More About...

Tyler would love to visit the Calgary Stampede. It's a famous rodeo held every July in Calgary, Alberta. Cowhands compete in many exciting events, like riding bucking broncos and roping calves. Ask your librarian to help you find out more about it. Talk to a friend about why you would like to attend the Stampede!

TECH LINK
Check the Internet for information.

Ranching Words

Here are some words from the story about ranching:

> **cattle, drive, herd, pasture,
> cowhand, trail, corral**

With a partner, discuss what these words mean. Use a dictionary if you need to.

Now write a paragraph telling what will happen to Tyler and Jessica next year on the cattle drive. Use these and other words from the story.

Something To Think About

In good stories, the main character learns something. By the end of the story, Tyler learns that some things are more important than having new boots. What do you think he learns?

WRITING IN YOUR JOURNAL

At the top of a page write, "I got what I wanted, but nobody noticed!" Then tell a story about yourself. Tell about a time you got what you wanted—but it didn't turn out the way you expected.

What kind of family do you have? Large or small? What do you and your family do together? How do you help each other?

The Place Where You Belong

Article by GRETCHEN SUPER   Pictures by KEES DE KIEFTE

Everyone you know lives in a family. Every family is different. Every family is a different group of people. But every family is the same, too.

A family is much more than just a group of people. It's where people love each other and take care of each other. It's where people share their lives together.

What kind of family do you have?

There are all kinds of families.

But no matter what kind of family you have, your family is the place where you belong.

Tasha

Tasha lives in two families. She lives with her dad and her stepfamily during the week. And she lives with her mom on the weekends.

Tasha explains it this way: "My mom and dad got divorced. After the divorce, my dad married someone else. She was divorced, too, and had a son of her own."

Tasha's stepfamily is called a blended family. In a blended family, people live together who used to live in other families. Tasha has a stepmother and stepbrother.

So now Tasha lives in two families. Sometimes she gets tired of explaining what kind of family she has. "If *you* think it's confusing," Tasha says, "think how *I* feel!"

It was very hard for Tasha when her parents decided to get divorced. She knew they were unhappy. They used to argue most of the time. The rest of the time, they hardly spoke to each other.

But Tasha wanted her family to stay together. She hated it when her mom moved to a new apartment.

When she was with her dad, she missed her mom. And when she was with her mom, she missed her dad.

"I felt like I was split in two," Tasha says. "But there was only one of me to go around."

It was even harder when her dad decided to get married again. Now she had two families. Now she had two mothers.

"I don't need a new mom," Tasha would say. "I already have one!"

But Tasha got used to living in two families. She really likes her stepmom. They painted Tasha's bedroom together. They made the ceiling look like a blue sky filled with white, puffy clouds. Tasha's stepbrother helped, too. He made a sign that said "Tasha" for her bedroom door.

Tasha likes to lie on her bed and look up at the sky. She knows that her mom and dad are happy now. She knows that they love her as much as ever.

"Besides," she thinks, "it's kind of fun to have two bedrooms." She has a "weekend bedroom" at her mom's apartment. "Only now I have two bedrooms to keep clean," Tasha adds.

Tasha spends part of each summer with her mother, too. They always go camping. This summer, they are going to the mountains. "The tent is my third bedroom," Tasha laughs.

Tasha likes living in her two families. They are the places where she belongs. ⬡

FOLLOW UP

Tasha lives in two families. Is her family like yours? Or is it quite different?

Understanding the Article

Family Feelings

- Why do Tasha's mom and dad live in different places?
- Why does Tasha feel "like I was split in two" after her parents get divorced?
- Why does Tasha feel confused after her father marries again?
- How many people are there in Tasha's family now?
- In the end, Tasha gets used to living in two families. What are some of the good things she does with both families?

Family Words

On the chalkboard, complete this chart by filling in the missing words. (Some of them are in the article.)

With your classmates, think of even more family words. Add them to the chart!

Family Words Chart

Males	Females
dad	mom
	stepsister
uncle	
	grandmother
nephew	

Write a Postcard

Do you have relatives who live out of town? Ask a grown-up at home to give you the address of a faraway cousin, aunt, or other relative. Then write your relative a postcard. Tell them about your summer holiday, what you're doing in school, or who your best friend is this year.

Don't forget to sign your name. Then write the address, stick on a stamp, and mail it!

A Paragraph

YOUR TURN TO WRITE

In your notebook, write about what your family is like.
Who are the members of your family?
What do you do with each family member?
How does each one make you feel?

Dear Aunt Yasoo,
Summer in Vancouver was the best!
I saw three whales and

Yasoo Raja
1010 Main Street
SASKATOON, SK
S7M 5L4

If We Didn't Have Birthdays

POEM AND PICTURE BY **Dr. Seuss**

If we didn't have birthdays, you wouldn't be you.

If you'd never been born, well then what would you do?

If you'd never been born, well then what would you be?

You *might* be a fish! Or a toad in a tree!

You might be a doorknob! Or three baked potatoes!

You might be a bag full of hard green tomatoes.

Or worse than all that…Why, you might be a WASN'T.

A Wasn't has no fun at all. No, he doesn't.

A Wasn't just isn't. He just isn't present.

But you…you ARE YOU! And, now isn't that pleasant.

Read It Aloud

Get together with six classmates to read the poem out loud. There are lots of ways to have fun with this poem! Here are some ideas:

- When funny words come along, act them out: "a fish," "a toad in a tree."
- Three people could say "three baked potatoes!"
- Everyone could shout the words in capital letters.

Add your own ideas. Practise reading slowly and clearly. Then present the poem to the class.

Invitations

Imagine the best birthday party you could have! Think about food, games, sports—anything you like. Then write and draw an invitation to your friends telling them all about the party.

MORE GOOD READING

❧ **Grandpa's Visit**
by Richard Keens-Douglas

A lonely young boy spends all his time with his TV and VCR—until his grandpa comes to visit.
(a picture book story)

❧ **Postcards Talk**
by Linda Granfield

Find out all about old and new postcards, what they should say, and how to collect them.
(a non-fiction book)

❧ **Waiting for the Whales**
by Sheryl McFarlane

A girl and her grandfather spend time together, gardening and watching the whales.
(a picture book story)

Tree

Poem by Frank Asch

If only I could stand
still enough, long enough,
with my arms in the air,
I'm sure I could become
a tree.
After a while my fingers would turn green
and my toes would turn down into the ground.
Every day I'd drink the sunlight
and taste the earth,
but then one day I'd scream,
"Hey, it's me!"
and I'd tell everyone
just what it was like to be
a tree.

Have you ever
planted a seed and
watched it grow?
This poem explains
how a plant grows.
The pictures and
words in the boxes
give you extra
information.

A Seed Grows
A First Look at a Plant's Life Cycle

Poem and Information by **Pamela Hickman**

Pictures by **Heather Collins**

This is the seed
that Sam planted.

Peek inside the seed to see where
the leaves and the root of the new
plant will come from.

This is the stem that grew from the seed that Sam planted.

Take a look at the world underground.

Can you find these creatures?

June bug grub

pupa

worm

ant

wireworm

tiger beetle larva

This is the flower
that bloomed on the stem,
that grew from the seed
that Sam planted.

Inside a bud is a new flower waiting
to bloom. Do you see other flowers
in the garden?

This is the bee
that drank from the flower,
that bloomed on the stem,
that grew from the seed
that Sam planted.

A bee laps up nectar with its tongue.

In the hive the nectar is made into honey.

nectar: a sweet liquid made in flowers (bees use nectar to make honey)

This is the pollen
that was left by the bee,
that drank from the flower,
that bloomed on the stem,
that grew from the seed
that Sam planted.

A bee collects pollen for food. The pollen sticks to a bee's hairy body, but some gets rubbed off on the next flower the bee visits.

This is called pollination. A flower must be pollinated before fruit can grow.

 This is the fruit
that was made with the pollen,
that was left by the bee,
that drank from the flower,
that bloomed on the stem,
that grew from the seed
that Sam planted.

A watermelon grows all summer, and then it is big enough to pick and eat. Look in the garden for more things that are ready to pick.

These are the new seeds
that formed in the fruit,
that was made with the pollen,
that was left by the bee,
that drank from the flower,
that bloomed on the stem,
that grew from the seed
that Sam planted.

Yum!

Peek inside the watermelon. It contains many new seeds. Each seed can be planted next year to grow a lot more watermelons. These other fruits and vegetables also have seeds that can be planted.

Do you have any questions about the way a plant grows? Write them in your notebook. Later you can check the library, or search the Internet, for more information.

Understanding the Selection

Life Cycle of a Plant

A cycle is a lot like a circle. The life cycle of a plant begins with a seed and ends with a seed!

This circle shows the life cycle of a plant. Copy it into your notebook. Then read the mixed-up sentences in the box.

Add them to the circle in the right order (the first thing that happens is number 1, and so on).

The first one is done for you.

Mixed-up Sentences

Pollination takes place.

New seeds grow inside the fruit.

The bud opens into a flower.

A seed is planted.

The fruit starts to grow.

Roots, stem, and leaves sprout from the seed.

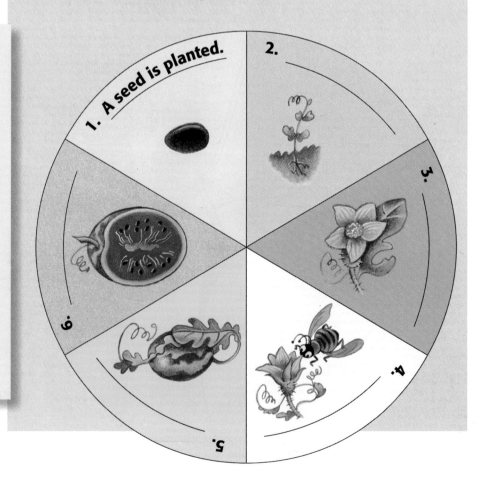

A Poem That Grows

Does this poem remind you of poems you've read before? Find a copy of the old poem, "This Is the House That Jack Built." How does the poem grow? Does Pamela Hickman's poem grow in the same way?

With a partner, try writing your own poem that grows. Choose one of these starting lines,  or make up your own!

This is the playground our town built.

This is the grass the cow ate.

Using New Words

How does a bee **pollinate** a flower? Look back at *A Seed Grows* to find out. Write this story in your notebook. Use words from the hive to fill in the blanks.

hive
nectar
pollen
female
fruit

The Busy Bee

Busy Bee visits a male flower and sips the sweet _____.

While Busy Bee drinks, _____ sticks to its hairy body.

Busy Bee flies over to a _____ flower. Pollen drops onto the flower.

Later, the flower turns into a round, ripe _____.

Meanwhile, Busy Bee goes back to the _____ to make honey.

PLaNt POWER

Will a plant grow toward light? Can beans crack plastic? Here are two experiments that will help you to find out. Read both of them carefully before you try them yourself.

Fun with plants from Dr. Zed

Experiments by Gordon Penrose

Experiment 1—Light Seekers!

Grow some light-seeking, hole-peeking beans.

YOU WILL NEED:

- a shoe box with a lid
- scissors
- water

- two dried kidney beans or navy beans
- soil

- a small container (small enough to fit in the box)

INSTRUCTIONS:

1. Cut a circle the size of a small juice can in one end of a shoe box.

2. Plant two dried navy or kidney beans in a small plastic container filled with soil.

3. Place the container in the end of the box opposite the hole.

4. Put the lid on the box and set it in a sunny place. Check it every day and water the beans every few days.

5. When your plant begins to peek through the hole, take off the lid to see how it grew. We've snipped away the side of the box to show you what happened.

Why do you think the plant grew through the hole?

Experiment 2—Pea Power!

True or false? Seeds have enough power to crack plastic.

Fill a plastic glass with dried peas or beans. Now add water up to the top. Cover the top tightly with plastic wrap and secure it with a rubber band. Wait a couple of hours for the cra-a-ack!

What are the answers: Will a plant grow toward light? Can beans crack plastic? When you do the experiments, do you think they will work in the same way?

Try the Experiments

Try experiment 1 first.
Work with a group of friends.
First, collect the materials.
Then follow the steps in order.
Ask an adult to help you if necessary.
   Now try experiment 2, at home or at school.

Understanding the Experiments

Explaining Why

- Did you follow the steps of the experiments in order?
  Why is this necessary?

- Did your plant grow through the hole?
  How many days did it take?

- What happened when you tried experiment 2?
  Why did that happen?

Now read Dr. Zed's Explanations on page 59.

A Record of Your Experiment

Copy this page into your notebook. Make notes about how you did experiment 1 or experiment 2. Be sure to include anything different about your materials, or your method. Add pictures to your record.

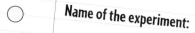

Name of the experiment:

Materials I used:

How I did the experiment:

Step 1:

Step 2:

Step 3:

Step 4:

What happened:

What I learned from the experiment:

Dr. Zed's Explanations

Here's how Dr. Zed explains the two experiments you did.

EXPERIMENT 1

Beans, like other green plants, need water and light to make food and grow. The only light in the box is through the hole at the end. So the beans grow in that direction.

EXPERIMENT 2

Seeds take in water, swell, and break open as they grow. As the beans get bigger, they need more room to expand. So they crack the plastic glass.

BEFORE READING

What are your favourite insects? Do you dislike any insects? Why?

Ladybug Garden

The gardener looked all around his garden, and he liked what he saw. There were hardy vegetables, brightly coloured flowers, and fruit trees that made the air smell sweet. There were many kinds of insects in the garden, too: ladybugs and wasps, bees and butterflies, aphids and ants.

Story and Pictures by **Celia Godkin**

The gardener thought about all those insects.
He knew that bees and butterflies helped the garden grow.
As they flew from flower to flower, drinking nectar,
they picked up a fine yellow dust called pollen,
which the flowers produced. By carrying pollen
from one flower to another, the bees and butterflies
helped the flowers produce seeds for new plants.

61

Though the butterflies were helpful, the gardener
knew that their young—the caterpillars—were not.
They often damaged plants by eating the leaves.

The ants and wasps in the garden were
harmful in one way but helpful in another.
They sometimes nibbled on ripe fruit
before the gardener got around to picking it.
But they also helped the garden
by eating harmful insects.

There was no question about the aphids, though. The gardener knew they were bad for the garden, because they sucked plant juices and spread diseases.

He didn't know much about the bright red ladybugs, but he thought they were special and was very fond of them.

One day the gardener had an idea. If I get rid of the bad insects, he thought, my garden will be perfect. So the next day, the gardener sprayed the fruit trees, the vegetables, and the flowers. He used a spray gun filled with bug killer.

As the gardener sprayed the poison, the bees, ants, and wasps hid in their nests to protect themselves. But the ladybugs didn't have any nests, so they flew away in a great red cloud.

The aphids didn't have nests either, but, without wings, they couldn't fly away. They hid under the leaves in the garden.

When the gardener finished spraying, the aphids
crept out of their hiding places and went back to work.
Many of them died from the poison, but others
survived.

The aphids sucked the juice out of leaves and tender
plant stems. Some of the juice passed through their
bodies and turned into a sweet, sticky liquid called
honeydew.

Soon it seemed there were more aphids than ever
before. As they multiplied, they sucked more and
more plant juice. It wasn't long before the plants in
the garden were coated with sticky honeydew,
which ants love.

There were so many ants going to get honeydew from the aphids that the gardener began to see ant trails all over the garden.

The bees in the garden liked honeydew, too. It was easier for the bees to lick honeydew from the plants to make their honey than it was for them to go from flower to flower collecting nectar. Besides, there were fewer flowers now. The plants had become too sick to make many flowers, because of the damage the aphids had done.

With fewer flowers, there were fewer butterflies visiting the garden. But there were still many caterpillars. They stayed in the garden, eating leaves, until they grew big enough to turn into butterflies and fly away.

Not only were the plants too sick to make many flowers, the fruit trees were too sick to produce much fruit. Wasps buzzed angrily about, fighting over what little fruit there was.

The gardener knew that something was terribly wrong. The garden had few flowers, the fruit trees had little fruit, and the vegetables were shrivelled up and wilted. The plants were covered with aphids.
There were ant hills and ant trails everywhere.
The wasps were becoming a nuisance,
and the butterflies had all but disappeared.
Even the bees' honey tasted strange, because they had made it from honeydew instead of nectar.

The gardener didn't know what to do.
He could see that spraying with poison had been a mistake. He understood now that all the life in his garden was linked somehow, that the plants and insects depended on one another to survive.

"What about ladybugs?" a friend suggested.

"What about them?" the gardener asked.

"Ladybugs are nature's way of controlling aphids," the friend replied. And she gave him an address from which to order a supply.

When the box of ladybugs arrived, the gardener took it out to the garden, opened it, and left it in a shady spot under a tree. One by one, the ladybugs flew or crawled out of the box. Soon they were all over the garden.

The ladybugs ate all the aphids they could find. They ate and ate and ate and ate. And after a while, the garden began to recover. The plants grew stronger and healthier.

When the following summer came, the gardener looked all around his garden. Once again there were hardy vegetables, brightly coloured flowers, and lots of sweet, ripe fruit. The butterflies were back. The ants and wasps had settled down. And the bees were making delicious honey. Everything was as it should be.

The gardener smiled. He had always known there was something special about ladybugs!

FOLLOW UP

What is the gardener's favourite insect? Why? What did you think of ladybugs before you read the story?

Understanding the Story

Harmful or Helpful?

- Why does the gardener spray bug killer on his garden?
- What do the ladybugs do when he sprays? What do the aphids do?
- What bad things happen when the aphids begin to multiply?
- When does the gardener see that spraying with poison was a mistake?
- How do the new ladybugs solve the problem?

Good reading— Now you're a bug expert!

Classify the Insects

Now that you have read the story, think about which insects are harmful to the garden and which are helpful. Copy this chart into your notebook. ➡ Add a check mark under the right heading on the chart. The first one is done for you. Remember, some insects are both harmful and helpful.

Insect	Harmful	Helpful
ladybugs		✓
wasps		
bees		
aphids		
ants		
caterpillars		

Balance of Nature

The gardener learns a lesson in this story.

> "He understood now that all life in his garden was linked somehow, that the plants and insects depended on one another to survive."

This means we have to keep a balance in nature. If we kill one kind of insect or animal, we will have too many of another kind. Can you think of examples? Discuss these ideas with your classmates.

Make Ladybug Crafts

Get together with a group of three or four classmates. Talk about how you could make big, colourful ladybugs from paper, cloth, sticks, stones, twist ties, or other materials. Make lots of them and create a ladybug display. Some could hang on strings, while others sit on green paper leaves.

Did you ever look at something and wonder if it was alive? Are stones alive? What about seashells? What about your hair?

Living Things

Experiment by **Adrienne Mason**

IS IT ALIVE?

Living things are all around you. They can be plants, animals, fungi, or tiny bacteria, but they all have some things in common:

- Living things are made of tiny cells. Cells are so tiny you need a microscope to see them. Your body has millions of cells, and so do plants and other animals.

- Living things need food, air, water, and a habitat (a place to live).

- Living things grow, reproduce, and respond to the environment around them.

There are seven living things on the previous page. Can you list them?

WORDS TO KNOW

bacteria: tiny plants made of one cell—some are helpful but others cause diseases

fungi: living things that are neither plants nor animals, such as mushrooms, mould, and yeast

reproduce: to produce offspring (plants reproduce using seeds)

chlorophyl: the chemical in plants that makes leaves green

photosynthesis: the way green plants use sunlight to make their own food

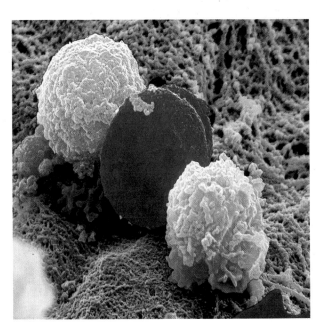

Red and white blood cells.

EGG HEADS
EXPERIMENT

You are full of water—it is in your blood, in your cells, even in your bones. All living things need water. But how much? Grow some tasty sprouts to find out.

YOU WILL NEED:
- a small nail
- three eggs
- three egg cups
- a bowl
- three cotton balls
- some alfalfa seeds (available in the bulk food section of grocery stores)

WHAT TO DO:
1. Using the nail, carefully make a hole about the size of a quarter in one end of each egg.
2. Hold the eggs over the bowl and let the insides drain out. (Use the insides for cooking.)
3. Put a cotton ball into each egg shell.
4. Sprinkle enough seeds on each cotton ball to cover it.
5. Add just enough water to one egg shell to moisten the cotton ball thoroughly. Fill the second egg shell with water so that the cotton and seeds are completely covered. Do not water the third egg shell.
6. Put the egg shells in a sunny place. Over the next week, keep the cotton ball moist in the first one and the seeds covered with water in the second one. Never water the third one. Which egg head grows the best sprout "hair"?

WHAT'S HAPPENING?

Like all living things, seeds need water to grow. The outer coating on the seed softens, and the roots, stems, and leaves begin to grow from it. But seeds can have too much water. In the egg with the most water, the seeds couldn't get any air, so they didn't grow.

In the picture on the left, which egg head do you think got just the right amount of water?

LIVING THINGS NEED WATER

The cells that living things are made of need just the right amount of water to work properly. Without water, living things will die. ⬡

Did you find seven living things on page 70? Check your answers below. How many non-living things did you find?

Try the Experiment

Try the Egg Heads Experiment.
Work with a group of classmates.
Collect the materials. Follow steps 1 to 6.
If you want, ask an adult to help you
with step 1.

- Did your experiment work well?
- How many days passed
  before the seeds sprouted?

Make a record of your experiment.
Use the same headings as you did on page 59.

Understanding the Experiment

Explaining Why

- Why do seeds need water?
- What happens if seeds get too much water?
- What happens if seeds don't get enough water?

ANSWERS

boy, girl, girl,
butterfly, plant, cat,
goldfish

Try Another Experiment

TATTOO A PLANT

Plants can't eat, so
they need to make
their own food.
How do plants do this?
Grow a plant and find out.

YOU WILL NEED:

- scissors
- cardboard
- three paper clips
- a young plant

WHAT TO DO:

1. Cut the first letter of your
   name, or any other shape, out
   of cardboard. This is your tattoo.
   Cut out three tattoos.
2. Paper clip a tattoo to the upper
   surface of the leaves of the plant—
   one tattoo per leaf.
3. Put the plant in a sunny spot
   and water it every other day.
4. After a week, remove the tattoos.
   What do the leaves look like?
   Wait a week. Now how do the
   leaves look?

WHAT'S HAPPENING?

The plant's leaves are like
mini-factories. They make food
using light, water, a gas called
carbon dioxide, and chlorophyl,
the chemical that makes leaves green.
This process is called photosynthesis.
When you covered part of a leaf
with the tattoo, light couldn't reach
the leaf, so food stopped being made
in that part of the leaf.

DISCUSS WITH YOUR CLASSMATES:

What would happen if you covered
the whole leaf with a tattoo?

Do you know what your five senses are? This article is all about the sense of taste. Read it and you'll find out some surprising facts.

ARTICLE BY
Pamela Hickman

PICTURES BY
Pat Stephens

How Sweet It Is

Are there foods that you really like and others you'd rather not eat? Wild animals also have favourite foods. Many caterpillars like only one kind of plant. Birds won't eat Monarch butterflies because of their bad taste. Cats can't taste sweet things at all.

Your taste buds are on your tongue. You may be surprised to find out what body parts other animals use for tasting.

If you were a butterfly...

- you would have taste buds on your feet. You'd walk around on a flower before deciding if it was good enough to eat.

- your tongue would be coiled up like a party blower under your head. To feed, your tongue would straighten out like a straw and suck up the flower's sweet nectar.

- you would be two hundred times more sensitive to sweet things than a human is.

How Your Tongue Tastes

Food comes in four flavours: sweet, salty, sour, and bitter. Your tongue tastes sweet flavours at the tip, salty flavours just behind the tip, sour flavours on the sides, and bitter flavours at the back.

One at a time, put a little sugar, salt, lemon juice, and powdered cocoa on your tongue. Can you tell where your tongue tastes them?

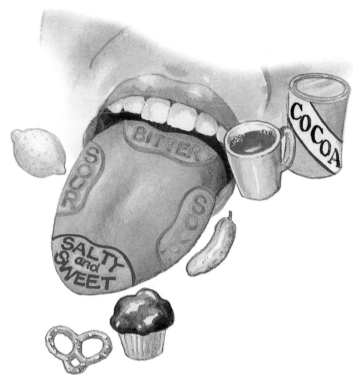

Caution: If you have any allergies or health problems, check with your teacher before trying this.

Tasting Without Tongues

- Butterflies, moths, and flies taste with their feet. Many other insects taste with their antennae.
- Mussels and scallops from the sea test their food with their tentacles.
- If you were a catfish, you could tell if something was good to eat by swimming close to it. How? Because your body would be covered with taste buds.

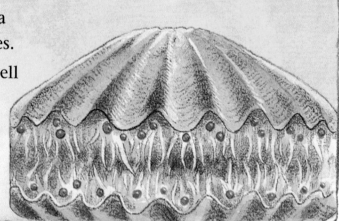

Check Out These Talented Tongues

Pour some milk into a saucer and try lapping it up the way a cat does. It's not as easy as it sounds. A **cat's** tongue is very rough so the milk "holds on" to the tongue as the cat drinks. Cats also use their tongues to clean and brush their fur.

A **giraffe's** tongue is protected from the sun while it picks leaves from the treetops. The tongue has its own natural sunscreen!

Woodpeckers have extra long, sticky tongues. They are perfect for catching insects for food.

Snails have "toothy" tongues for shredding plants before eating them.

Lizards use their tongues to clean their eyes.

A **toad's** tongue is attached at the front of its mouth. That's so it can flip out a long way to catch a tasty fly.

What was the most surprising thing you learned about taste in this article? Which creature has the most useful tongue, in your opinion?

Understanding the Article

Tasty Tasters

- Why do you think different animals (including humans) like different foods?

- What are the four basic flavours of food we eat?

- Why do you think butterflies taste with their feet? What other body parts do insects and sea creatures use to taste things?

- What animals in this article have special tongues? Why do these animals need special tongues?

Find Out More About...

If you like butterflies, you can attract them to your garden. Butterflies like special flowers and shrubs. Kids in some elementary schools have built butterfly gardens. Ask your librarian for help finding information on butterflies. Search the Internet, too. Then draw a plan for a butterfly garden.

TECH LINK
Use a drawing program to help you prepare your plan.

Classifying Foods

Below is a chart of Food Flavours. Copy it into your notebook. At right is a list of foods with different flavours. See if you can place each kind of food under the right heading on the chart.

Sweet	Salty	Sour	Bitter

Discuss your answers with your group.
Do any foods fit in more than one category?
Which foods were the hardest to place?
Can you add two more foods to each category?
Which category has the fewest foods?

ice cream
potato chips
steak
doughnuts
unsweetened chocolate
lemons
radish
broccoli
cola drinks
fudge
popcorn
rhubarb
coffee

OUR TURN TO WRITE

A Tasty Tale

What would happen if people could taste with their elbows? or hear with their feet? or see with the back of their heads? Invent some characters with "crazy senses." Then write a story about what happens to them!

MMMM

Bugs! Bugs!

Nonsense Poem by **Jack Prelutsky**

Pictures by **Steve Attoe**

Bugs! Bugs!
I love bugs,
yes I truly do,
great big pink ones,
little green stink ones,
yellow bugs and blue.
I put you in my pockets,
and I wear you in my hair.
You are my close companions,
I take you everywhere.

Bugs! Bugs!
I love bugs,
any shape or size,
thin ones, fat ones,
long ones, flat ones,
bugs with bulging eyes.
I hug you and I kiss you
and I bounce you on my knee.
No matter what I'm doing,
my bugs are close to me.

Bugs! Bugs!
I love bugs,
bugs you are my friends,
square ones, round ones,
half a pound ones,
bugs with big rear ends.
I love to watch you scamper,
and I love to watch you chew.
I've got no doubt about it—
bugs, I'm bugs for you!

Spaghetti Seeds

Nonsense Poem by **Jack Prelutsky**

"These are the best spaghetti seeds,"
the farmer promised me.
"And each of them will grow to be
a fine spaghetti tree."

I planted them a year ago...
that farmer is a phony.
I've not got one spaghetti tree—
just fields of macaroni.

A Nonsense Poem

Bugs! Bugs! and *Spaghetti Seeds* are nonsense poems. That means they make no sense (or not much sense!).

Try writing your own nonsense poem based on Jack Prelutsky's poems.

1. What do you love—scary things? icky food? mud puddles? Celebrate them in a poem like *Bugs! Bugs!*

OR

2. What if you planted an alarm clock? your report card? a hockey puck? What would grow? Think of some crazy ideas, then write your "seed" poem!

Make a Spaghetti Garden

Pasta comes in all sorts of amazing shapes! With your group, collect a variety of dry pasta. Find a large piece of poster board. Then arrange the pasta to make flowers, trees, or insects. When you've completed your design, glue the pasta to the paper. You can colour or paint it, if you like.

Display your "spaghetti garden" for the whole school to see.

MORE GOOD READING

The Kids Canadian Plant Book
by Pamela Hickman
Open this book and find beautiful pictures and interesting facts about plants across Canada.
(a non-fiction book)

Wild in the City
by Jan Thornhill
From butterflies to bats, you can find all sorts of wild animals in cities, and in this book.
(a non-fiction book)

The First Red Maple Leaf
by Ludmila Zeman
An amazing tale about why maple leaves first started to turn red. (a picture book story)

Bringing the Rain to Kapiti Plain
retold by Verna Aardema
In this pattern story, young Ki-Pat helps the plants grow again by bringing rain to the plain.
(a picture book story)

Winter Weather Watch

POEM BY **Robert Heidbreder**

What weather's in the West today?
Snow, snow—come what may!

And on the Prairies? Out that way?
Snow, snow—buckets they say!

And by the Great Lakes? Round there, eh?
Snow, snow—without delay!

And in Québec what's under way?
Snow, snow—a white soufflé!

And in the Maritimes today?
Snow, snow—in every bay!

But what about up north, I say?
Snow, snow—it's there to stay!

Dig out your skis, snowshoes, your sleigh,
Your slick dogsled,
Go out and play!

Kids Canada

BEFORE READING

Can you imagine walking on the ocean floor, under the ice? That's what Eva does, alone for the very first time, in this story.

Story by
Jan Andrews

Pictures by
Ian Wallace

Padlyat:
Paddle-ee-AH

Very Last First

E va Padlyat lived in a village on Ungava Bay in northern Canada. She was Inuit, and ever since she could remember she had walked with her mother on the bottom of the sea. It was something the people of her village did in winter when they wanted mussels to eat.

Today, something very special was going to happen. Today, for the very first time in her life, Eva would walk on the bottom of the sea alone.

Time

Eva got ready. Standing in their small, warm
kitchen, Eva looked at her mother and smiled.

"Shall we go now?"

"I think we'd better."

"We'll start out together, won't we?"

Eva's mother nodded. Pulling up their warm hoods,
they went out.

Beside the house there were two sleds, each
holding a shovel, a long ice-chisel, and a mussel pan.
Dragging the sleds behind them, they started off.

Eva and her mother walked through the village. Snow lay white as far as the eye could see—snow, but not a single tree, for miles and miles on the vast northern tundra. The village was off by itself. There were no highways, but snowmobile tracks led away and disappeared into the distance.

Down by the shore they met some friends and stopped for a quick greeting.

❄ ❄ ❄ ❄

They had come at the right time. The tide was out, pulling the seawater away, so there would be room for them to climb under the thick ice and wander about on the seabed.

Eva and her mother walked carefully over the bumps and ridges of the frozen sea. Soon they found a spot where the ice was cracked and broken.

"This is the right place," Eva said.

After shovelling away a pile of snow, she reached for the ice-chisel. She worked it under an ice hump and, heaving and pushing with her mother's help, made a hole.

Eva peered down into the hole and felt
the dampness of the air below. She breathed deep
to catch the salt sea smell.

"Good luck," Eva's mother said.

Eva grinned. "Good luck yourself."

Her eyes lit up with excitement and she threw
her mussel pan into the hole. Then she lowered herself
slowly into the darkness, feeling with her feet until
they touched a rock and she could let go of the ice
above.

In a minute, she was standing on the seabed.

Above her, in the ice hole, the wind whistled.
Eva struck a match and lit a candle.

The gold-bright flame shone and glistened on the wet stones and pools at her feet.

She held her candle and saw strange shadow shapes around her. The shadows formed a wolf, a bear, a seal sea monster. Eva watched them, then she remembered.

"I'd better get to work," she said.

Lighting three more candles, she carefully wedged them between stones so she could see to collect mussels. Using her knife as a lever, she tugged and pried and scraped to pull the mussels off the rocks. She was in luck. There were strings of blue-black mussel shells whichever way she turned.

Alone—for the first time.

Eva was so happy she started to sing. Her song echoed around, so she sang louder. She hummed far back in her throat to make the echoes rumble. She lifted up long strings of mussels and let them clatter into her pan.

Soon her mussel pan was full, so she had time to explore. She found a rock pool that was deep and clear. Small shrimps in the water darted and skittered in the light from her candle. She stopped to watch them. Reaching under a ledge, she touched a pinky-purple crab. The fronds of the anemones on the ledge tickled her wrist.

Beyond the rock pool, seaweed was piled in thick, wet, shiny heaps and masses. Eva scrambled over the seaweed, up and onto a rock mound. Stretching her arms wide, tilting her head back, she laughed, imagining the shifting, waving, lifting swirl of seaweed when the tide comes in.

The tide!

Eva listened. The lap, lap of the waves sounded louder and nearer. Whoosh and roar and whoosh again.

Eva jumped off the rock, stumbled—and her candle dropped and sputtered out. She had gone too far. The candles she had set down between the stones had burned to nothing. There was darkness—darkness all around.

"Help me!" she called, but her voice was swallowed. "Someone come quickly."

Eva closed her eyes. Her hands went to her face. She could not bear to look.

She felt in her pockets. She knew she had more candles there, but she could not seem to find them.

The tide was roaring louder and the ice shrieked and creaked with its movement.

Eva's hands groped deeper. She took a candle out at last and her box of matches, but her fingers were shaking and clumsy. For a long, forever moment, she could not strike the match to light the candle.

The flame seemed pale and weak.

Eva walked slowly, fearfully, peering through the shadows, looking for her mussel pan.

At last, she found it and ran stumbling
to the ice hole. Then, looking up, Eva saw
the moon in the sky. It was high and round
and big. Its light cast a circle through the hole
onto the seabed at her feet.

Eva stood in the moonlight. Her parka glowed.
Blowing out her candle, she slowly began to smile.

By the time her mother came, she was dancing.
She was skipping and leaping in and out of the
moonglow circle, darkness and light, in and out.

"Eva," her mother called.

"I'm here," she called back. "Take my mussel pan."
Eva scrambled onto a rock and held the pan up high
to her mother. Then her mother's hands reached down
and pulled her up, too, through the hole.

Squeezing her mother's hand, Eva saw the moon,
shining on the snow and ice, and felt the wind
on her face once more.

"That was my last very first—my very last first
time—for walking alone on the bottom of the sea,"
Eva said.

FOLLOW UP

Would you like to have an adventure like Eva's? What is the most exciting thing that happens to her?

Understanding the Story

Under the Ice

- Why do the people in Eva's village walk on the bottom of the sea? What season do they choose for this?

- Why do Eva and her mother wait for the tide to go out before they walk on the seabed?

- What sea creatures does Eva see when she's walking under the ice?

- Why does Eva get scared?

- At the end of the story, what does Eva mean when she says, "That was my very last first time"?

Reading a Map

Eva lives on Ungava Bay in northern Canada. Can you find Ungava Bay on a map or a globe? Look on the northern coast of Québec.

- What shape is Ungava Bay? What towns or villages can you see?

- What is the "vast northern tundra" like? Check your library for information.

TECH LINK
Check the Internet for information. Use the search words **Ungava Bay**.

A Letter

Imagine that Eva is your pen pal. Write her a letter about yourself. Ask questions about her adventure. Include a story about the very first time you did something exciting. Share your letter with a friend.

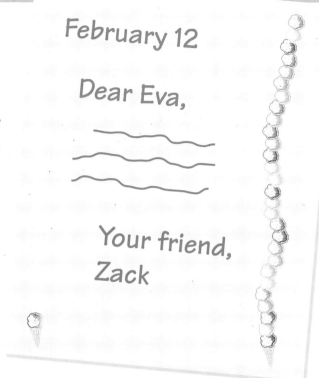

February 12

Dear Eva,

Your friend,
Zack

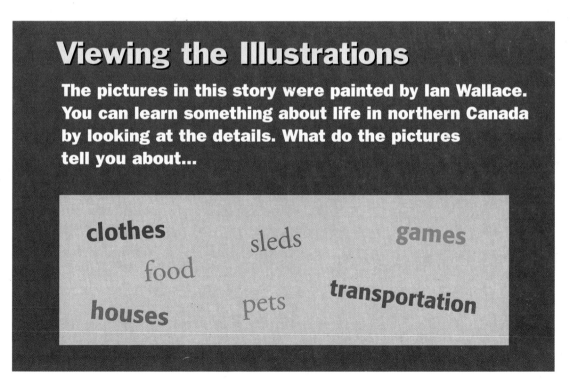

Viewing the Illustrations

The pictures in this story were painted by Ian Wallace. You can learn something about life in northern Canada by looking at the details. What do the pictures tell you about...

clothes   sleds   games

food

houses   pets   transportation

WHO HiDeS iN tHe PaRK?

Text and Pictures by
Warabé Aska

Come visit Stanley Park! You'll find it in Vancouver, British Columbia. The park is almost surrounded by the Pacific Ocean. You can bike around it on the seawall. Among the giant trees hide Beaver Lake, the Lost Lagoon, and a miniature railway. It's a wonderland for kids!

Animals—half human, half god—hide in the great totem poles.
The killer whale, lord of the sea, and the wolf,
lord of the land, are linked by the frog.
But in the air above them all, the raven reigns
as Creator God, source of light.

It is one of the oldest trees in the world, perhaps 1000 years old.
Was it man or god who hollowed it out?
Was it done by fire or lightning?
Once horses, carriages, and cars drove into it.
Today children hide in it.

Who Hides in the Park?

At the end of the day, when buildings across the water light up like stars,
children take some of the magic home with them.
But they also leave a little of themselves to join all the other
spirits hiding in the park.

Viewing the Illustrations

The artist, Warabé Aska, sees fun, beauty, and magic in special places like Stanley Park. What do you see in his paintings? Can you find...

- children turning themselves into totem poles?
- a hollow tree?
- children flying with the seagulls?

What colours does Warabé use for each painting? How do the different colours make you feel? What magic things do you see in his paintings?

Create a Mural

Every park in every town has special places to see. One fine day, go out with your classmates to visit your local park. Each of you choose a special spot, and draw a sketch of it. Try to include birds, animals, and kids in your pictures. When you get back to school, paint your pictures in colour onto a big classroom mural.

Find Out More About...

Have you heard of skiing at Whistler? West Coast native art? hiking on Vancouver Island? British Columbia has beautiful beaches and mountains, and exciting things for kids to do. Find out more about them at your library or on the Internet.

Write a one-page report. Include a paragraph on each of the following:

- places to visit
- things to see
- things to do

Name three different places you have visited in Canada. What provinces are these places in?

Messages by
Canadian Kids

Postcards
Canada

Signpost on the Trans-Canada Highway, Victoria, BC.

Dear Alain,

This car trip is so-o-o long. We're on the longest road in the world—the Trans-Canada Highway. It's over 7500 km long, from St. John's, Newfoundland, to Victoria, British Columbia. Did you know that Canada is the second largest country in the world? Only Russia is bigger.

Yours truly,
Michelle

P.S. Mom told me that Canada's name comes from the Huron-Iroquois word *kanata*, meaning "village." Pretty big village!

ALAIN DESJARDINS
110 RUE MARCEL APT 1048
LAVAL QC   H7P 3X9

Dear Lenore,

I had a blast at the Calgary Stampede. Many different First Nations groups marched in the big parade. I saw a rodeo event every day for ten days. The best was the bronco riding and the steer wrestling. I bought you a cowboy hat.

Yours truly,
Alexis

First Nations member at opening
of the Calgary Stampede, Calgary, AB.

LENORE CRESTWATER

WAHPETON DAKOTA

FIRST NATION

PRINCE ALBERT SK S6X 1A3

Dear Chris,

This morning we arrived in Churchill, Manitoba. It was much colder than it looked— -15˚ C. The polar bears were hard to spot. After more than an hour, I saw my first polar bear! He was only a hundred metres away from me!

Your friend,

Jenna

P.S. Churchill is known as the polar bear capital of the world.

CHRIS YEE
3236 EAGLE RIDGE CRES
CRANBROOK BC V1C 6K9

Polar bear outside Churchill, MB.

Canola fields in Saskatchewan.

Dear Rajiv,

Yesterday we arrived in the sunniest place in Canada—Estevan, Saskatchewan. Of course the sun was out. I expected to see nothing but wheat fields in Saskatchewan. But there are lots of bright, yellow crops—that's canola. We're going to see the Big Muddy Badlands tomorrow.

Bye for now,
Carly

RAJIV ASSURIAN
52 BLUEFOX RD NORTH
LETHBRIDGE AB T1H 6E6

Victoria, BC, at dusk.

CANADA

Dear Jake,

Victoria is great! I can't believe how warm it is here in February. We've been to Butchart Gardens and the Royal British Columbia Museum.

See you soon,
Stefan

P.S. Mom says that tomorrow we'll go whale watching. Maybe we'll see some otters, too.

JAKE SANTOS
189 CRYSTAL DRIVE
FREDERICTON NB E3B 9B8

Dear Ira,

We visited the annual blueberry festival in Cumberland County, Nova Scotia. The wild blueberries were the best thing I've ever tasted. Dad told me that the schooner on the Canadian dime, the *Bluenose*, was built in Lunenberg, Nova Scotia. It used to be the fastest ship in the world.

Yours truly,

Brian

IRA DAWES
4242 DENNIS ST APT 12
BRANDON MB R7A 5G7

The *Bluenose*.

Dear Theo,

There's so much to see in Toronto. We had a hard time deciding what to visit first. I wanted to go up the CN Tower—the tallest building in the world—but we took the ferry over to Centre Island instead. It was fun biking there because there are no cars allowed on the island. I found out that Toronto's main street, Yonge, is the longest street in the world.

Your friend,
Shanti

THEO POULOS
2795 GEORGE ST
SYDNEY NS B1M 1B1

Train on Centre Island, Toronto, ON.

Bonhomme in a calèche,
Québec City, QC.

Dear Kala,

We went for a very slow carriage ride through
the streets of Québec City. The driver told us
that it's the oldest city in Canada and the only
walled city in North America. Most people
speak French here. I learned how to say "cool"
in French.

Yours truly,
Lisa

P.S. Dad found a building that was built
in 1658, and people are still living in it.

KALA SEKLAR
432 RAINBOW RD
WHITEHORSE YT Y1A 5E2

Have you visited
any of the places
named in the
postcards? Which
place would you
most like to visit?

Long Distance Conversation

Work with a partner. One of you plays the part
of one of the postcard writers. The other plays
himself or herself.

Now imagine that you are talking to each
other by long-distance telephone.
Ask each other questions
about where you live, or
places you have visited.
Answer as well as
you can!

A Treasure Hunt Postcard

This game is for the whole class.
Bring a small gift from home and hide
it in the playground. Make a postcard
and write a message on it telling how
to find the gift. Put all your postcards
in a big box, shuffle, and pick a new
card. At recess, look for the hidden
treasures!

Reading a Map

Here is a map of Canada. The dots mark the places named in the postcards. In your notebook, write the place names listed in the box. Beside each name, write the number of the dot that shows where the place is. Add one fact you learned about that place.

Estevan

Calgary

Québec City

Churchill

St. John's

Toronto

Lunenberg

Victoria

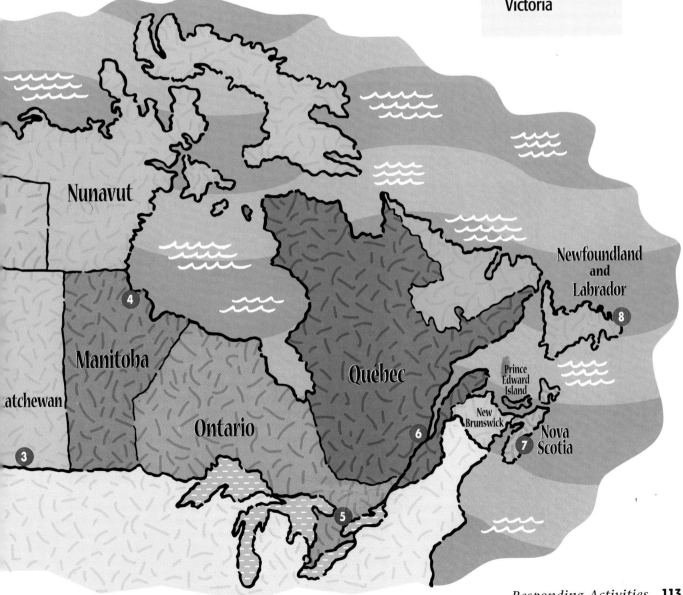

This story begins, "When I was a boy..." This tells you that the story took place many years ago–perhaps thirty or more– when the man telling the story was young. Enjoy his adventure!

The Fishing Summer

Story by
Teddy Jam

Pictures by
Ange Zhang

When I was a boy my three uncles lived in a big wooden house by the sea. Every summer they painted it white. They had white shirts, too. On Sundays they would do the laundry and hang their white shirts out on the line, where they would flap in the wind like big raggedy gulls.

My three uncles and my mother had been children in that white wooden house. Every summer my mother would take me there for a visit.

My uncles had a fishing boat. It was like a huge rowboat with a little cabin in the middle, hardly big enough to go inside. At the end of the little cabin was the engine.

That engine had started off in a big car. Uncle Thomas, who was the oldest and had a long black beard, had taken the engine out of the car and put it in the boat. Even when it rained and stormed, Uncle Thomas could keep the motor going.

Uncle Rory was the middle uncle. His beard was black, but he kept it short by cutting it with the kitchen scissors. He could look at the sky and tell if it was safe to go out. And when the wind blew up the sea, and the clouds and fog fell over the boat like a thick soupy blanket, Uncle Rory could find the way home.

Uncle Jim was the youngest uncle and my mother's twin. He had no beard at all. He was the fisherman. He had to know where the hungry fish would be, and what they would be hungry for.

At the end of each day I would stand at the dock, waiting. The boat would come in, and my uncles would pick me up. Then we would go to the fish factory. There I would help my uncles load the fish into cardboard boxes to be weighed on the big scale. A giant with little eyes that looked like bright fox eyes would write down the numbers on a piece of paper. Then my uncles would take the paper to the cashier and get paid.

I wanted to go fishing.

"One day," Uncle Jim said, "when you get big."

"No way," my mother said. "You'll fall in and drown."

"I can swim," I said.

"You're only eight years old," my mother said.

"I started going when I was eight," said Uncle Thomas out of his big beard.

"Thomas," said my mother in a sharp voice that made the room go quiet. And I remembered another story. That my grandfather used to fish with his own brothers, and when one of the brothers got hurt, Thomas took his place. A few years later he dropped out of school and started fishing all year round. When my grandfather drowned, my other uncles started going out on the boat with Thomas.

My Fishing Adventure

That night I couldn't sleep. I wanted to go fishing so badly. I got dressed, then went down to the dock.

All along the bay you could hear the waves gently splish-splashing, the boats swaying and creaking against the docks. The stars were huge and bright. They hung over the sea like fruit ready to fall.

I stepped from the dock into the boat. It was strange being there alone. I wondered what it would be like to pull off the ropes, drift across the ocean and end up in some country I'd never even heard of.

The rocking of the boat made me sleepy. I went into the cabin and pulled an old blanket over myself.

I woke up to the sound of the motor hammering in my ears. I pushed back the blanket and scrambled out of the cabin. We were at sea!

But the boat was barely moving. My uncles were hauling in huge nets. Soon the boat deck was covered with narrow flopping herring twice the length of my hand, shining and silvery in the sun.

The whole time they emptied the nets into the boat, my uncles pretended I wasn't there, looking right past me, or stepping around me.

Suddenly Uncle Jim pointed at me and shouted, "Stowaway!"

The others looked as though surprised to see me. "Stowaway. Aye, Captain. Throw him overboard."

For just the tiniest little moment I wasn't sure what was going to happen. Then they all laughed and rumpled my hair and patted me on the back as though I'd done some wonderful thing.

"Your mother knows you're here and we promised not to drown you," said Uncle Rory, handing me a knife. "Now all you have to do is earn your keep."

The herring were the bait. I helped Rory cut them up while Thomas headed the boat out past the mouth of the cove. That was the farthest I'd ever been. I could still see my uncles' house, a small patchy white square against the wild heather and grass.

Soon even the cove's mouth had disappeared from view. My uncles drank tea with milk and sugar from their thermoses. They also had a thermos for me. It was filled with hot chocolate. And in the little plastic lunch suitcase my mother had prepared for us was a bag of cookies.

"You see?" Rory said. "You did bring us good luck."

I put my hands in the sea to wash away the fishy smell. In the water my fingers looked white and dead. They came up numb with the cold, and I had to slap my hands together to warm them up.

The waves were going slip-slap against the boat. With each wave the front of the boat rose up. Then it fell down into the trough before the next wave carried it up.

"Feeling sick?"

"I'm fine," I said.

"I always used to puke," Rory said. "Then I started drinking tea. Keeps my stomach down."

"We didn't want to tell you this before you came," Thomas said, "but he might still puke any time. Better stay out of his way." Thomas's big black beard made it hard to know when he was joking.

Suddenly in the middle of the ocean, when we could hardly see the land any more, Thomas stopped the boat and threw down anchor. He baited a hook for me, and I began letting out my line.

The idea was to let it right down to the bottom of the ocean, pull it up a bit, then jig it up and down. In those days millions of cod were parked at the bottom of the ocean, waiting for lunch. When I felt something on the line, I was supposed to wind it up.

The first couple of times I didn't have a fish at the end.

"There's currents at the bottom," Rory told me. "They feel like a fish at first. Wait for a bigger tug."

I waited. I kept getting tugs, but I didn't know if they were bigger. Finally I pulled up the line again. At the end was a huge lump. It was so big I thought it must be a rubber boot. But it turned out to be a fish.

Rory swung it into the boat. It landed with a big thump and just lay there. Thomas attached it to a stringer and put it back in the water.

Meanwhile my uncles were hauling fish up as fast as their arms could go. I kept catching them, but slower. My hands grew sore and red.

Thomas found a greasy old pair of gloves from beside the motor.

"Didn't have gloves when we were boys," he said.

"Nope," said Rory. "Dad made us stick our hands in vinegar to make them tough."

On the way back, just outside the cove, we stopped to set the herring nets again. "That way there'll be something here for us tomorrow," Rory explained.

Suddenly he whirled and threw the net out of the boat. It spread into a giant billowing mesh, then slowly settled on the water. But one of the corners got tangled up. Thomas eased about around the net, then as we came close, told me to lean over and grab the wooden float.

As I did, a little wave came up under the boat. A tiny little wave you wouldn't notice unless you'd been stupid and leaned over so far that when the wave came and the boat tipped you slid off the boat into the water.

The water was colder than ice. It filled up my shoes, put its fingers between my toes, quickly soaked my pants and started to drag them down.

I began swimming hard, kicking with all my strength, but I forgot to shout. The boat was moving away when I finally called out. My uncles turned around and saw me in the water.

Thomas cut the motor and Rory held out the paddle to me. I was too proud of my swimming to use it. I splashed right up to the boat, then reached up and grabbed the gunwale.

When I got out, I felt like my fingers had looked— white and numb. Rory grabbed the greasy blanket I'd slept under and wrapped it around me. Then he sat me on his knees and squeezed me till I got warm.

My Mother Fights Back

We were one of the first boats home, but my mother was down at the dock, waiting for us. I had taken off the blanket, but my soaking clothes told my mother I'd been in the water.

"How did that happen?" she demanded, glaring at my uncles.

"Now, Edith," Uncle Rory said. The same tone he'd used one Christmas when he caught her cheating at cards.

"Just tell me."

"It was my fault," I said. "I was leaning over the side of the boat and I just fell in."

"Swims a lot better than you used to," Uncle Thomas said. *"He's a natural."*

He's a natural. Uncle Thomas's voice when he called me that was the purest praise I'd ever heard. He wasn't just saying I was a good swimmer, or a good kid for taking the blame. He was saying I was part of the family. A real fisherman, like him and Rory and Jim and my grandfather's father. Right then, if he had just asked me, just snapped his fingers, I would have jumped in the ocean and swum forever.

My mother's face turned red again. We walked up to the house. She had made a big old-fashioned tea with cookies and cakes and sandwiches to celebrate the first day fishing.

I went upstairs to change, then came down to eat. "Well," Thomas said to my mother, "aren't you going to be asking him if he enjoyed himself? Now that he's a member of the crew."

"Don't be giving me that," my mother said. "You can wait a few years. Until then he does his swimming in pools and at the beach."

"Don't be making him a baby," said Uncle Rory.

"He's a fisherman now," Jim said.

"He is not!" my mother shouted. "He *is* a baby. He's my baby and you're lucky you didn't drown him."

Uncle Thomas was standing at the counter refilling his cup. Uncle Jim just sat there, looking at my mother as though she were a stranger. Rory, too. The news was coming onto the radio with that funny little crackle it had.

I looked at my mother. She turned away from me. Now my uncles started staring at their feet, as though they'd been caught wearing girls' socks.

"I want to go," I said.

"You're not going anywhere," my mother pronounced.

The next day I was out on the boat again. My uncles were hauling up fish faster than ever. So was I, because my mother was there, helping me.

It was a hot day, and when we got back to the cove the water felt warm on my hand. My mother put her own hand in, to test it. Rory and Thomas were standing at the front of the boat, their big tanned arms folded across their chests, satisfied with the day's work. My mother went and stood between them.

"Great day," she said.

"It was," Rory said. "To tell you the truth, Edith, I didn't know you had it in you."

"Thanks," my mother said. She had her hands on her brothers' backs. Then she gave a push. They hit the water with a giant double splash. I was the one who had to pull them in with the oars.

My mother was laughing so hard, she couldn't move.

From that day we both went out with my uncles every day. By the end of the summer my arms had new muscles and my hands were tough as canvas. On the last day my uncles grabbed my mother and tossed her in. She wasn't even surprised. She just took off her boots, heaved them toward the boat, then swam to shore.

It was the last evening before we had to go back for the start of school. My uncles had caught some lobsters, and that evening we roasted them in a fire on the shore.

Then they toasted me and said how I'd become a real fisherman. Uncle Thomas gave me a drink of his coffee. It was bitter and it was raw and it was sweet. It was the taste of that summer and I never lost it.

Now the fishing factory is closed. Uncle Rory and Uncle Jim moved to the city and got married. Uncle Thomas still lives in the old house. He runs a car repair garage that also sells newspapers and rents videos. My mother still goes to see him when she can.

After hundreds of years of everyone's grandfather and grandfather's grandfather going out to sea, no one in the village fishes any more. The fish are gone. At night you hear them talking about it on the radio and television. There are lots of words, but no fish.

This fishing adventure happened long ago. But at the end of the story, something has changed. What is that change?

Understanding the Story

Fishing Fun

- Why doesn't the boy's mother want him to go fishing with his uncles?

- How does the boy fall out of the boat? What should he have been wearing?

- How does the boy feel when Uncle Thomas says he's a natural?

- Why is the boy's mother annoyed with her brothers? Does she have good reasons?

- At the end of the summer, the uncles call the boy a "real fisherman." How do you think he feels?

Tell an Anecdote

People feel proud when they learn to do something well. When does the boy in the story feel proud? What do you feel proud of?

Get together with a partner to tell an anecdote (a true story about yourself). Make it about a time when you felt proud of something you were able to do. Then listen carefully as your partner tells you a story!

WRITING IN YOUR JOURNAL

On the last page of the story there is a powerful message. What is it? What do you think happened to the fish?

Imagine that you are Uncle Thomas. Write about how he must feel now that there are no fish to catch.

Fishing Words

float: a floating object that can hold up a fishing line

gunwale: the top edge of the side of a boat

jig: to pull a line with fish hooks up and down

stowaway: a person who hides on a ship or airplane to get a free ride

stringer: a chain with hooks for keeping fish you've caught

Plan a Visit

If you could go to an Atlantic province, what would you take with you? What would you like to see? What would you like to eat?

Get together with a partner. Ask the adults at home for ideas. Visit the library, too. Then transfer these drawings into a notebook and fill in the spaces with your ideas.

What I'll Take

What I'll See

Menu

What I'll Eat

The Circle of Thanks

Song collected by Joseph Bruchac
Mi'kmaq, Northeast Coast

As I play my drum
I look around me
and I see the trees.
The trees are dancing
in a circle about me
and they are beautiful.

As I play my drum
I look around me
and I see the sun and moon.
The sun and moon are dancing
in a circle about me
and they are beautiful.

As I play my drum
I look around me
and I see the stars.
The stars are dancing
in a circle about me
and they are beautiful.

As I play my drum
I look around me
and I see my people.
All my people are dancing
in a circle about me
and my people, they are beautiful.

Personal Response

- In the poem, the trees, the sun, the stars—everything is dancing. What do you think this means?
- What is the drummer thankful for? Are you thankful for the same things, or different things?
- Would you rather be a drummer or join the dancers? Why?

Creative Movement

Join hands with your classmates to make a large circle. Walk or dance around the room. One of you might play a drum!

Four students then go into the middle and form a new circle. Each one reads one verse of the poem, while turning and "looking around."

MORE GOOD READING

🍁 **At Grandpa's Sugar Bush by Margaret Carney**

In this story, a young boy helps his grandfather make maple syrup, and then enjoys some pancakes. (a picture book story)

🍁 **Eenie Meenie Manitoba by Robert Heidbreder**

In these "Playful Poems and Rollicking Rhymes," the poet crosses Canada from coast to coast. (a poetry anthology)

🍁 **The Long Road by Luis Garay**

The story of José's journey to a new country—Canada. (a picture book story)

Just Stories

Open a Book

Poem by **Jane Baskwill**

Open a book
And you will find
People and places of every kind;
Open a book
And you can be
Anything that you want to be;
Open a book
And you can share
Wondrous worlds you find in there;
Open a book
And I will too,
You read to me
And I'll read to you.

**B E F O R E
R E A D I N G**

Do you ever feel
that small people
need to stand up
to bigger people?
Have you ever
done this? What
happened?

*Tale from India
retold and
illustrated by*
Jan Thornhill

Elephant and Hare

Hare and her friends had always lived peacefully
among the tall grasses that grew on the shore
of a clear blue lake. No one ever bothered them.

One day Elephant came crashing out of the jungle,
followed by his herd. The elephants were thirsty and
had been looking for water for a long time. When they
saw the shimmering blue lake, they were so excited,
they stampeded through the grasses toward the water.
They were in such a hurry, they didn't notice that they
were trampling the burrows of Hare's friends beneath
their huge feet.

After drinking and washing, Elephant led his herd
back into the jungle to spend the night. On their way,
the elephants' enormous feet crushed many of the
tender grasses that Hare and her friends used for food.

Hare was frantic with worry. She knew the elephants
would return to the lake the next day, and the hares'
homes and food would be destroyed completely.
She thought very hard and finally came up with an idea.

"Don't worry," she told the other hares. "I have
a plan."

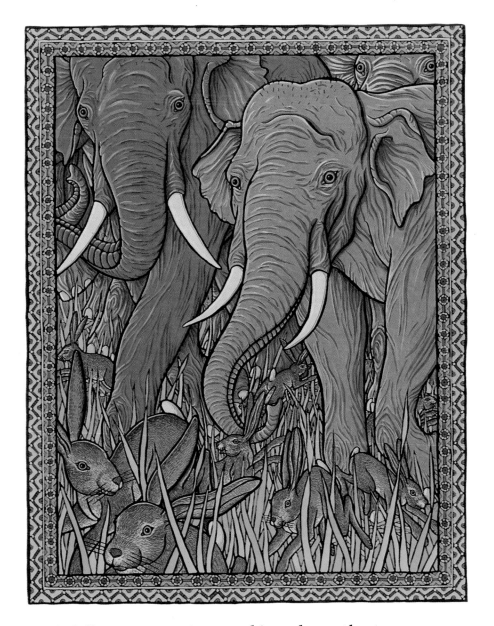

A full moon was just peeking above the trees
as Hare hopped to the jungle to talk to Elephant.
She hopped right into the middle of the herd and
started shouting as loud as she could, but no one paid
any attention to her because her voice was tiny and
hard for elephants to hear. When Hare was almost
hoarse with shouting, Elephant flapped his ears.
He thought there was some kind of strange insect
buzzing around his head. He flapped his ears again,
but the noise wouldn't go away.

"What's that annoying sound?" he finally said.

"It's me!" shouted Hare.

Elephant looked down. He squinted at Hare and said, "Who are you?"

"I am a loyal subject of the all-powerful moon god," said Hare, bowing. "He has sent me to give you a message."

"Go on," said Elephant politely, although he didn't believe a word Hare was saying.

"When you and your herd went down to the lake today," said Hare, trying not to sound nervous, "you trampled the homes and food of the moon god's loyal subjects. This has made the moon god extremely angry. He is so angry that he commands you to leave and never return."

"I don't believe in any moon god," scoffed Elephant. "Give me proof."

"Follow me to the lake then, and you will see the moon god for yourself," said Hare. "But watch where you're walking this time," she added.

When Elephant and Hare got to the edge of the lake, Hare pointed at the reflection of the full moon in the still water.

"There is the mighty moon god," she said. "Pay your respects by dipping your trunk in the lake."

Elephant thought this was a silly thing to do, but he agreed. He stretched out his long trunk and touched the surface of the lake with it. Instantly, the water quivered and rippled, making the moon's reflection burst into hundreds of shimmering pieces. Elephant threw back his trunk in fright.

"See how angry the moon god is?" shouted Hare.

"You're right," said Elephant, shaking with fear. "I promise I'll never annoy the moon god again!"

And with that, Elephant headed back to his herd in the jungle, being very careful indeed not to step on any grasses or burrows on his way. ⬡

FOLLOW UP

Do you think Hare is brave and clever in this story? How does she know that Elephant will be afraid of a creature who's even bigger than himself?

Understanding the Tale

Hidden Strength

- What problem do the elephants cause for the hares? Do the big animals notice what they are doing?
- How does Hare show how brave she is?
- Does Elephant believe in this "all-powerful moon god" at first?
- What does Hare do to convince Elephant that there really is a moon god?
- How does Hare trick Elephant in the end?
- Which is more powerful in this story: size or brains? Explain your answer.

Action Words

Elephants are big, active animals. Jan Thornhill uses lots of action words to show what elephants do:

crash   stampede   trample   crush

Can you think of two action words to show what each of these animals do?

- a parrot
- a snake
- a moose
- an elephant being careful "not to step on any grasses or burrows"

A Small and Big Story

Write your own story about a small character who stands up to a big one. First, choose your characters. It could be an ant and a person, a mouse and a giraffe, or better— your own idea.

Then make three cartoon drawings of:

1. a problem that happens between them

2. how the small character plans to trick the big one

3. how it all works out

Finally, write your story. Help your small character to find its hidden strength. Have fun!

You Be the Judge

CHARACTERS

Elephant and Hare are the two main characters in this story. Things happen in the story because of the way they act. Is one of them bad and the other good? You decide!

1. Elephant tramples the Hares' burrows and grasses.

   Is he (a) mean, or (b) careless?

2. Hare makes a plan to stop Elephant from destroying things.

   Is she (a) clever, or (b) sneaky?

3. Elephant thinks a shattered reflection means the moon god is angry.

   Is he (a) crazy, or (b) gullible? (Gullible means easily deceived.)

Now get together with a partner. Do you agree with each other? Convince each other you're right by giving good reasons for your opinions.

BEFORE READING

Kitoto is a young mouse who goes looking for a powerful friend to protect him. Find out who he meets!

How to say the names:

Kitoto:
Key-toh-TOH

Kigego:
Key-geh-GOH

Savannah:
the African Savannah is a large grassy plain, with just a few trees here and there

KITOTO THE MIGHTY

Tale from Africa by **Tololwa M. Mollel**
Pictures by **Kristi Frost**

High in the sky, a hawk circled and searched. Then, swift as an arrow, he dropped to the ground.

Barely ahead of the hawk's claws, Kitoto darted into a bush. The little mouse who had never learned to dig burrows hid there, with nothing to eat all day.

The next morning, before the sun was up or the hawk awoke, Kitoto scurried hungrily across the Savannah. He found a fallen baobab fruit. But another creature had seen it first, and the delicious seeds were gone.

That is when the hungry little mouse heard the sound of a big, rushing river. Cautiously, he approached the river bank and watched the angry water sweep away huge trees and rocks.

"How powerful the river is!" thought Kitoto. And he had an idea.

"I am Kitoto the Mouse, small and weak," he cried to the river. "I wish to make friends with you. With a friend like you to protect me, I won't have to go hungry for fear of the hawk. You must be the most powerful of all beings."

"Not so," roared the river. "The sun can protect you better for he is far more powerful than I. He burns me to a trickle in the dry season. The sun is the most powerful being."

The river wove a beautiful nest of steam, placed Kitoto inside, and gently blew it above the trees and mountains, into the soft sunlight.

"Why, I am bigger than the Savannah!" Kitoto marvelled, as the earth below grew smaller and smaller. He felt very pleased with himself. Still, he had never in his life imagined making friends with one as powerful as the sun.

"I must do my best to impress him," Kitoto decided, as he arrived at the sun's home late in the day.

Sparks swirled as the weary sun stoked and fanned his dying log fire.

Kitoto puffed himself up importantly. "I am Kitoto the Mighty, Master of the Savannah," he announced. "I wish to make friends with the most powerful being. I thought it was the river. But no, the river tells me it is you."

The sun, wrapped in a blanket, shivered in the chill of dusk. "Not so," he replied. "There is one far more powerful than I, who gathers the clouds and hides the Savannah from my view. The wind is the most powerful being."

In the morning, the sun sent Kitoto across the heavens on a beam from a fresh log fire. Kitoto peered at the Savannah, small as a nut, far, far below, and felt very grand indeed.

He found the wind hard at work, tugging the clouds together. "I am Kitoto the Great, King of the Savannah," he declared. "I wish to make friends with the most powerful being. I thought it was the river, who told me it was the sun. But no, the sun tells me it is you."

"Not so," replied the wind. "There is one far more powerful than I, one I cannot tug with my strong braids, however hard I try. The mountain is the most powerful being."

With the longest of her braids, the wind swung Kitoto away to a distant mountain peak.

"I am Kitoto the Magnificent, Emperor of the Savannah," the little mouse proclaimed to the mountain. "I wish to make friends with the most powerful being. I thought it was the river, who told me it was the sun, who told me it was the wind. But no, the wind tells me it is you."

"Not so," thundered the majestic mountain. "There is one far more powerful than I, who chomps away at my root. Surely this creature, whom I have felt but never seen, must be the most powerful being of all."

Then the mountain rumbled and opened wide, allowing Kitoto to enter.

Down, down Kitoto scampered, through dark pathways, deep to the root of the mountain. There, he found himself in a huge maze of tunnels, archways, halls, and chambers. The walls were cool and smooth and smelled pleasantly. Tiny, shiny pebbles lit the way.

At every bend, Kitoto expected to see a giant loom before him, for a giant it must be, he thought, to carve such a world out of the mountain.

A sound from the shadows startled him.

In his fear, Kitoto forgot to be Mighty or Great, Master, King, or Emperor. "Please do not harm me," he pleaded with the unseen giant. "It is only Kitoto the Mouse, small and weak. I wish to make friends with you, the most powerful of all beings. With you to protect me I won't have to go hungry for fear of the hawk." Kitoto waited, trembling.

From the shadows, a figure stepped forward.

Kitoto stared in amazement as the figure bowed.

"I am Kigego, the mountain mouse. Welcome to my home."

"*Your* home? You built all this?" Kitoto asked. "The paths, the tunnels...*everything?*"

"Everything," replied Kigego. "With nothing more than my teeth and a lot of hard work." Her eyes glowed proudly. "Come."

Like old friends, the two mice explored the winding pathways. They enjoyed a game of hide-and-seek in the mazes. They played catch with shiny pebbles. Then they fell asleep on cushions of soft earth.

When they awoke, Kigego unearthed a sumptuous hoard of bulbs, tubers, and roots. "I'll teach you the secrets of the ground," she promised, chuckling.

Kitoto chuckled back and said, "And I will teach you the secrets of the Savannah."

High in the sky, a hawk circled and searched. Deep at the root of a mountain, two friends chewed merrily away. And after the hawk had gone to sleep, they ventured out to enjoy the sweet, cool night air.

To this very day, few would guess that the mouse
is the most powerful being on the big, wide Savannah.
But the rushing river, the weary sun, the tugging wind—
even the majestic mountain, will tell you this is so.

**FOLLOW
UP**

How many
powerful friends
does Kitoto meet?
Which one turns
out to be the most
helpful? Were you
surprised?

Understanding the Story

Make a Story Map

Kitoto takes a long journey to find a powerful friend to protect him. Reread the story to remind yourself where he went in his travels.

Now take a large piece of paper. You are going to draw a "map" of the story to show Kitoto's journey.

First, use a pencil to plan where you will put everything. Then make a colourful drawing of the journey. Add a few words to make Kitoto's journey clear.

Share your map with a partner.

**Congratulations!
You followed Kitoto on
a very long journey!**

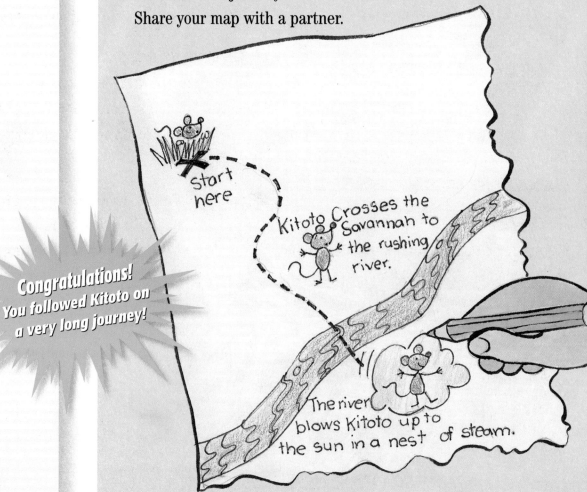

Write a Story

Write a story about a small character who meets a large and powerful character.

Who will your **audience** be? A group of younger kids, your family, or…?

1. Make an Outline

Make notes that answer these questions. Your notes will become your **outline**.

- What will your characters be like?
- What problems will your small character face?
- Where and when does your story begin?
- How does your story end?

2. Write a First Draft

Use your outline to write your story. Your **first draft** may change later.

3. Peer Review

Ask a partner to read your story and answer these questions:

- Are the characters described well?
- Is the story clear?
- What changes would make it more exciting?

4. Revise Your Story

Read your story out loud to yourself. What would you like to add or change? How can you make the story more exciting? Now rewrite your story. Include your partner's suggestions.

5. Proofread Your Story

Ask a partner to proofread your story, looking for mistakes in spelling and grammar. Check these things yourself, too.

6. Publish and Share

Correct your mistakes. Type your story into a computer or print it neatly. Add pictures to your story. Read your story to friends or family.

TIP When you write a story, it helps to write about what you know. For example, the small character in your story could be you. The problems the character has could be similar to problems you've faced.

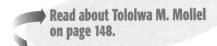

Read about Tololwa M. Mollel on page 148.

Tololwa M. Mollel

Profile by Michael Boughn

You may be wondering, "How does the author of *Kitoto the Mighty* know all about the creatures of the Savannah?" The answer is, "Because he grew up in Africa, where the story takes place!"

Tololwa Mollel lives in Canada now—in Edmonton, Alberta. So it was easy for me to phone and ask him lots of questions: "What was your childhood like? How did you become a writer? When did you come to Canada?"

We even chatted on e-mail!

Let's begin with his childhood. Tololwa grew up in two homes. The school close to his parents' house in Tanzania had only grades one and two. So, when he was eight years old, he moved 160 km away to stay with his grandparents on their coffee farm. He attended grade three in the nearby school. He lived with his grandparents for many years.

Why did Tololwa become a writer? He says it's because stories flowed all around him. His grandmother liked to tell stories before supper. The cooking took so long that she needed to keep the kids awake till the food was ready. His grandfather told stories all the time, too. But there were hardly any books around.

Tololwa told me, "I didn't own books till I started school. Then I fell in love with them." His favourite books were *Treasure Island* (all about pirates) and *Robinson Crusoe* (about a man who was shipwrecked on a desert island). "For a long time," Tololwa says, "I wanted to be a pirate and have my own island when I grew up."

Tololwa has lived in Canada for over fifteen years now. He isn't crazy about the cold winters in Edmonton, but he likes Canada because it is easier to be a writer here.

When Tololwa began to write his own stories, he often started with the old stories he learned at home. "Some of my stories are based on the folk tales and myths of the Maasai people in Tanzania," he explains.

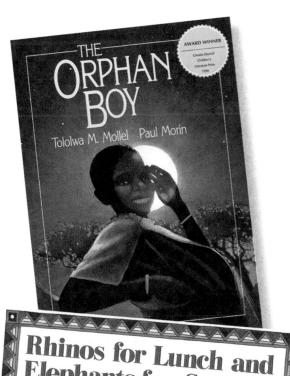

The Maasai are cattle herders. When Tololwa was writing his story *Song Bird* he remembered their exciting tales about monsters. "I decided to make my very own special type of monster: a milk monster. As I worked on the story, I remember thinking that cattle herders like the Maasai would be very worried about milk monsters. But in Canada, milk monsters aren't very scary." So Tololwa sometimes changes his stories to make them more interesting to kids who live here.

The story that inspired him to write *Kitoto the Mighty* is called *The Wedding of the Mouse*. Later, he discovered that there are many versions of this story, including one from Japan. In Tololwa's version, the mice don't get married, but they become very good friends!

Find out if everyone in your class knows the story of *Cinderella*. If not, take turns telling the story to them. Include as many details as you can!

Fairy Tale Spoof and Pictures by **Janet Perlman**

Cinderella Penguin

or, The Little Glass Flipper

There once was a young penguin named Cinderella, who lived in a faraway land with her stepmother and two stepsisters. Cinderella was a kind and gentle penguin, but her stepsisters were selfish and vain. Cinderella did all the chores. She even had to pick up after her stepsisters, while they never had to do a thing.

The sisters wore the finest of clothes and slept in large, cozy feather beds with silk sheets and fluffy pillows.

Poor Cinderella wore nothing but worn-out tatters and slept in the cold, stone cellar, up on a small shelf beside some old tin plates.

One day it was announced that the Penguin Prince was giving a costume ball. The stepsisters and their mother received an invitation. Cinderella wanted to go, too, but they just laughed at her.

"The Prince would never want to meet a shabby cinderblock like you!"

For weeks the house was filled with talk of the ball. The sisters had costumes made from the finest fabrics. They ate only the tiniest meals so they could have the tiniest waists, and they were always in front of the mirror, posing and practising their curtsies.

Finally the night of the ball arrived. Cinderella rushed about, ironing her stepsisters' costumes and helping them dress. Then, without a thank-you or goodbye, the carriage swept the stepmother and stepsisters off to the ball.

Cinderella burst into tears; she felt so alone and unhappy.

Suddenly, in a glow of blue light, the Great Fairy Penguin appeared before her.

"Why are you crying, Cinderella? Do you want to go to the ball?" she asked.

Cinderella blinked back her tears. "Oh yes, more than anything!"

"Then you shall!"

"First," said the Fairy Penguin, "you must fetch me a pumpkin from the garden."

Cinderella didn't know how a pumpkin could help her get to the ball, but she quickly brought her the best one she could find.

The Fairy gave it a firm tap with her wand, and it magically turned into a beautiful golden carriage.

Then the Great Fairy Penguin went into the kitchen and found six mice carrying a huge chunk of cheese. With a tap of her wand, they turned into a handsome team of six horses. She turned the cheese into a fat coachman in uniform. They all marched out the door and took their places, as if it were the most natural thing to do.

"Now you can go to the ball! Are you happy, Cinderella?" asked the Fairy.

"Oh, yes," said Cinderella. But then she looked sadly down at her ragged clothes.

"Oh, I almost forgot!" said the Fairy.

And with a tap of her wand, Cinderella Penguin's rags became a beautiful gown with gold trimming and a real gold tiara. On her feet were a pair of glass flippers, the prettiest and most delicate that Cinderella had ever seen.

Now, one last thing," said the Great Fairy Penguin. "The magic spell ends at the stroke of midnight. The carriage will turn back into a pumpkin, the horses back into mice, the coachman into cheese, and you'll again be dressed in rags. So you must leave the ball before midnight."

Cinderella promised to remember. Then, waving goodbye, she stepped into the carriage and rode off, her heart filled with joy.

When Cinderella arrived at the palace, the ball was in full swing. She was welcomed with a fanfare of trumpets and she marvelled to see so many fine penguins wearing such magnificent costumes.

Her stepmother and stepsisters didn't notice her. They were too busy gobbling down snacks and party sandwiches at the buffet tables.

But the Penguin Prince noticed Cinderella at once.

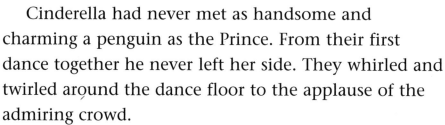

"Who is she?" he asked his courtiers. "She is the most beautiful penguin I have ever seen."

Cinderella had never met as handsome and charming a penguin as the Prince. From their first dance together he never left her side. They whirled and twirled around the dance floor to the applause of the admiring crowd.

"Who is the beautiful young penguin who has captured the Prince's attention so completely?" everyone whispered.

"What a handsome couple! How well they dance together!" they sighed.

Cinderella had never been so happy. She wished the night could last forever.

Then, suddenly, she glanced up at the clock. In all the excitement, she had completely forgotten the Fairy's warning.

"Oh!" she cried. "It's almost midnight. I have to go!"

And she ran from the palace in such a hurry that one of her glass flippers fell off and was left lying on the steps.

As Cinderella rode away in her carriage, the Prince called out, "Oh, please don't go!"

But she was gone.

He picked up the glass flipper and said sadly, "Who was she? I don't even know her name."

The next day it was announced that the Prince would marry the penguin whose foot fit the little glass flipper. There was great excitement throughout the land. First, all the princesses tried it on and then all the penguins of the court, but the flipper was always too small.

The royal footmen were commanded to take the flipper from house to house.

The stepsisters spent the whole day perfuming and powdering their feet.

"Cinderella," said the stepmother. "Your clothes are too ragged to be seen by the royal footmen. Go downstairs and polish the silver until they leave."

"Oh, please, I would like to try on the flipper, too!" said Cinderella, knowing it would fit her perfectly.

The stepsisters laughed, but then they looked down at Cinderella's webbed feet. For the first time they noticed how delicate they were.

A knock came at the front door.

"Quick! Hide her!" said the stepsisters.

They grabbed Cinderella, threw her down the cellar steps and slammed the door.

Poor Cinderella. She lay upside down with her foot caught tight in the door, unable to get free.

When the footmen came in, the stepsisters pushed and shoved to be the first to try on the flipper. They were so intent on snatching the flipper from each other that it slipped from their grasp, flipped high in the air, and landed squarely on Cinderella's foot!

Everyone stared. It was a perfect fit.

As the footmen opened the door and helped Cinderella up, the Great Fairy Penguin appeared. With a tap of her magic wand, she transformed Cinderella's tattered rags into the magnificent clothes she had worn to the ball.

Cinderella was overjoyed. "Oh thank you, Fairy Penguin! I thank you with all my heart!"

The stepmother's and stepsisters' beaks dropped wide open. They stared at Cinderella, spluttering with amazement.

"Look! Oh my!"

"It's her! Oh no!"

"Oh dear! We've really put our foot in it!"

The Penguin Prince and Cinderella Penguin were married the very next day, and the wedding bells rang throughout the land. Never before could anyone remember such a joyous and happy wedding.

Cinderella and the Prince truly loved each other and they lived happily together ever after.

FOLLOW UP

Did you enjoy the "penguin" version of Cinderella? What was the funniest part, in your opinion?

Understanding the Fairy Tale

That's Ridiculous!

What's ridiculous about these parts of Janet Perlman's story?

- The penguin stepsisters eat the tiniest meals so they can have the tiniest waists.
- The Great Fairy Penguin flies in the air.
- Cinderella wears a pair of glass flippers to the ball.
- When the footmen come, the stepsisters flip the flipper into the air and it lands on Cinderella's foot.
- The stepsisters say, "Oh dear! We've really put our foot in it!"

Viewing the Illustrations

The wonderful pictures in *Cinderella Penguin* were painted by Janet Perlman. Look for these funny details in her illustrations:

- penguin "mice" carrying cheese
- Cinderella's glass flippers
- penguin "horses" pulling Cinderella's carriage
- the costumes at the Prince's ball—a fish skeleton, an Egyptian mummy, and many more
- Cinderella and the Prince rock-and-rolling at the ball
- the penguin kids (and eggs) in the last picture

A Penguin Fairy Tale

Janet Perlman said to herself, "What if Cinderella and everyone else in the story were penguins? How would that change the story?" Then she wrote a funny version of the well-known tale.

You can do the same. Think of another well-known fairy tale. For example:

The Three Little Penguins

Snow White Penguin and the Seven Little Penguins

What funny things would happen? Write your story, then ask a friend to read it. Write it again, making it even better. Then draw some pictures to go with it. Take it home to read to your family!

MORE GOOD READING

🍁 **The Emperor Penguin's New Clothes**
by Janet Perlman
From the author of *Cinderella Penguin* comes another wacky Penguin fairy tale. (a fairy tale spoof)

🍁 **Crow and Fox**
by Jan Thornhill
This book has great illustrations and fun, short tales from around the world. (tales)

🍁 **Little Fingerling**
by Monica Hughes
This is the story of a very tiny boy, and how he succeeds in the big world. (a folk tale)

Ziggy Piggy and the Three Little Pigs
by Frank Asch
This book gives that old tale—*The Three Little Pigs*—a new and clever twist. (a fairy tale spoof)